The Digital Journey *in* K-12 Education

Overcoming Roadblocks and Embracing Innovation

Alan R. Shark

Executive Editor and Contributing Author

Written by leading professionals working the front lines of education

PUBLISHED BY THE PUBLIC TECHNOLOGY INSTITUTE • WASHINGTON, DC

Library of Congress Cataloging—Publication—Data

Shark, Alan R.
The Digital Journey in K-12 Education—
Overcoming Roadblocks and Embracing Innovation

ISBN-13: 978-1544841052
ISBN-10: 1544841051

1. Education—Effect of technological innovations—United States.
2. Educational technology—United States. 3. Education innovation—
United States. 4. Public schools—United States. I. Title

Public Technology Institute
660 North Capitol Street NW, Suite 400
Washington, DC 20001
www.pti.org

Contents

Acknowledgements

This is the second book in a series which began over a breakfast meeting in 2013 when I had the pleasure of meeting Renee Patton, head of Cisco's Public Sector Education efforts. We discussed the rapidly changing technology landscape that touches every aspect of education today. Thus, a seed of greater collaboration and innovation was planted that ultimately led to the publishing of both books.

The first book, *The Digital Revolution in Higher Education,* was a great success. Building on this success, it made sense to expand to what is happening in K-12 education. Like its predecessor, this book aims to explore technology and innovation in K-12 though the lenses of many different perspectives.

I am most grateful to Renee and her team, a wonderfully supportive and highly motivated group including Dr. Cynthia Temesi, Victoria Ryan, and Dr. Greg Mathison, Sr. This book has been a great collaboration between the Public Technology Institute (PTI) and Cisco, where PTI had full control of all editorial design and content.

Recognition and gratitude must also go to Keith Krueger and Marci Giang of the Consortium for School Networking (CoSN). CoSN is the premier professional association for school district technology leaders. Working with Keith and Marci was simply terrific, and they were instrumental with securing three of the 15 chapters. (To learn more about the many programs and services please visit www.cosn.org)

Of course, I am most grateful to all 15 authors who took the time to write and share their experiences. Without their insights and first-hand experiences this book would not be possible.

I am also grateful to PTI's expert production team, which includes Dr. Milena Ristovska and Sally Hoffmaster. Milena served as our copy editor who in her own right is a brilliant researcher. Sally is PTI's senior graphic designer. She has received many awards for art and design and created all cover designs and page layout for all PTI books and publications—both print and e-reader versions.

About Public Technology Institute (PTI)

Located in Washington DC area, Public Technology Institute was founded in 1971, and continues to actively support technology leadership for the public sector—state and local government and more recently, higher education. The mission is carried out through thought-leadership publications, research, education services, executive-level consulting services, training and certification programs, as well as awards and recognition programs. PTI also offers online educational programs throughout the year, and enjoys a dynamic relationship with Rutgers University's Center for Government Services. For more information, see www.pti.org.

Introduction

This is the second book in a series; the first is *The Digital Revolution in Higher Education*. Building on the former book's success, it made sense to expand the discussion to K-12 education with the recognition that this environment is different in many ways. The largest difference has much to do with how public institutions are governed. Higher education institutions total about 4,000 which includes 2-year colleges, while K-12 has over 98,000 schools. And historically K-12 schools are mostly governed locally with various funding challenges. The purpose of this book is to explore the state of digital technology and innovation in K-12, an evolution as opposed to a revolution. And we have done this though many different perspectives from experts who share a passion for education.

We have come a long way since the days when Apple was handing out hundreds of thousands of Apple 2 computers to schools throughout the country. Teachers were not as accepting of these new machines as they would be today. Software was scarce to non-existent, so we had hardware in search of software and meaningful applications. Of course, today there is no shortage of either. Contemporary challenges include how technology can enhance learning, and the growing worry that our young are more comfortable looking at a screen than looking into someone's eyes to communicate. Similarly, many would prefer texting to a one-to-one conversation with someone in the next room. And technology with all its great promise can also lead to social alienation plus bullying, and social discord.

Addressing an education summit in the spring of 2016 Bill Gates said "…that despite years of technology-infused innovation, the ed-tech industry has not really lived up its transformational promise." Given all the technology investments in K-12 schools, this warning may surprise some but with high school graduation rates at only 83%, and key test scores lagging other advanced countries, there is clearly more work to be done. Gates called for more engagement and longer-term planning among teachers and students—as opposed to responding to and focusing on technologies looking for a market. More specifically, technology must refocus more on addressing specific needs as identified by the consumers of educational technology.

This book is a thought and action collective with shared visions that provide practical ideas for future advancement. This digital journey is designed to be thought-provoking as it examines important considerations in the realm of K-12 education and technology, including perspectives from the educator/innovator, the teacher, the administrator, and the technology manager/leader. Each of the authors recognizes the obstacles and roadblocks that remain and focus on many positive opportunities and helpful examples.

We start our journey with *Redesigning the Learning Experience in the Digital Age* by Gabe Soumakian, a retired Superintendent who is passionate about supporting school districts through digital learning transformation. Since 2000, he has continued to serve as a cadre member of the Technology Information Center for Administrative Leadership. We conclude our journey with the very insightful *Digital Equity is the Civil Rights Issue of Our Time* by Keith Krueger and Jayne James, both with the Consortium for School Networking (CoSN). CoSn is regarded as the premier professional association for district technology leaders. They remind us of the urgent need to address technology—not just in the classroom, but in the home. Data clearly supports their argument: the digital divide between those with and those without home access to broadband and technology has grown worse over time.

Paul Russell provides the perspective of the CTO and shares his experience regarding his own journey that continues to unfold in a Connecticut school district. Bobette Sylvester-McCarroll, Assistant Superintendent for Business and Support Services for the Mesa Public Schools, shares her experiences from the practical and business side of technology implementation. Renee Patton, who has served as a teacher and school trustee, is currently the leader of Public Sector Education at Cisco and provides a framework for overcoming roadblocks and embracing innovation. Marie Bjerede, an established authority on mobile learning, is a Principal for Mobile Learning and Infrastructure at CoSN. Marie provides a useful four-step approach that recognizes that digital transformation is not an end goal, but rather it is a beginning. By creating a robust technology and human infrastructure, districts are creating not a final end-state, but a platform for continual evolution.

Dennis Fazio, an electrical engineer by training who has spent decades designing computer systems and components of the Internet, now spends his time supporting educational technology systems and community organizing in the Twin Cities of Minnesota. He points out that understanding the costs and assessing the value of a district's information technology (IT) environment and any proposed technology projects is vital if you, the technology leader, want to have credibility with your school board, Chief Financial Officer, superintendent, and community.

No discussion about the digital journey is K-12 would be complete without addressing the issue of "change." Greg Mathison, Jr. and Stephen Hankins serve respectively as Head Principal and Associate Principal at Marquette High School in the Rockwood School district, Saint Louis. They describe how great leaders empower teachers to innovate and take risks to reach their students' needs in the digital world. Leaders help the early adopters get the support they need to be successful via encouragement, professional development, and freedom to take educational risks. Change becomes contagious as teachers see their peers have success with new ideas.

James G. Lengel has worked as a teacher, educational leader, and university professor for 46 years, and is the author of nine books plus many articles on education and technology. His chapter is designed to help the school leader lead a school to reinvent itself to take full advantage of digital technologies for teaching and learning. It is based on the experience of dozens of schools and districts, and illustrated with examples from Denver, Colorado, and Rochester, New York. These districts mounted collaborative efforts to reinvent themselves, by imagining what a day in the life of a student should look like, publishing this vision to the community, and then using it as a source for planning and implementation.

Technology innovation requires not only leadership and vision, but it also requires sound governance. In her chapter, Leslie Wilson, CEO and co-founder of One-to-One Institute, believes education leaders cannot stand on the sidelines and allow obstacles to divert attention from educators trying to do the right thing with learners. Her chapter is a call to action for those who govern local, district, state, and national education organizations. Leslie points out that now is the time to understand and retool expertise to effectively lead schools today and into the future.

When information and instructional technology leaders communicate and collaborate, great things can happen. Mel Pace served in several capacities over his 45-year career and has been responsible for the visioning, planning, and implementation of numerous 21st Century technology initiatives. He is best known for his ability to get various groups and departments to collaborate and cooperate for the completion of intricate projects. In theory, the vision for a school district is set by the Superintendent, which may be true for the general vision but all too often is not what happens. In Mel's vast experience, visionary leaders who became Superintendents simply lose the capacity for vision. He believes it has to do with the daily stress of the politics of running a school district and provides some valuable lessons on how best to navigate the turbulent forces that are always present.

Driving change in workforce management is another variable to understand. Linda Misegadis, Public Sector Industry K-12 Expert at Kronos, and a former payroll director along with Rob Tibbs, also with Kronos, has a strong public sector background specifically with 12 years in K-12 education. Both Linda and Rob discuss how the demand for technology in the classroom continues to rise while the administrative support systems used by the workforce often get left behind. They point out that while new technology comes with costs, it also brings areas of efficiency, productivity, and visibility. How can technology bring a positive change to aging processes and ultimately contribute to student success?

When it comes to TelePresence, audio and video conferencing, the quality of communication and collaboration not only matters—it is essential. Jeff Billings is the IT Director at the Phoenix, Arizona, Paradise Valley Unified School District (PVUSD), and has been with them for 17 years. With a mission of cultivating world-class thinkers, the district knows that high-quality video and audio are critical to the success of both student education and to their business operations. Jeff writes that when one can communicate beyond text or audio, many more innate human traits are brought to bear, and authentic communication improves significantly. When communication improves, collaboration improves. When collaboration improves, problem solving capabilities improve.

A strong proponent of the "flipped classroom," Jon Bergmann is a chemistry teacher and one of the developers of the "flipped classroom" model of teaching. Jon decided to "flip" what students did in his classes, watching video lectures at home, and doing exercises (homework) in class under supervision. Flipped Learning at its core is a very simple idea. Students interact with introductory material at home prior to coming to class. This usually takes the form of an instructional video created by the classroom teacher and replaces direct instruction in the class, which is often referred to as a lecture. Then class time is repurposed for a variety of tasks such as projects, inquiry, debate, or simply working on class assignments that in a more traditional class would have been sent home. This simple time-shift is transforming classrooms across the globe.

So, as you can see, this book is indeed a journey into the K-12 digital learning environment. As editor, I intentionally left each of the authors to their own "voice," and it is my sincere hope that their voices will inspire you or re-affirm what you already know and believe. And quite possibly a chapter or two will take you by surprise, thus allowing you to rethink what you already thought you knew about how K-12 education is evolving and where we are going from here.

1

Redesigning the Learning Experience in the Digital Age

Dr. Gabe Soumakian

The American education system is ripe to experience one of the most exciting times to educate students and adults. We are at a moment in history where the acceleration of a rapidly changing world is impacting every facet of our lives and our economy. In order to succeed in a competitive workforce, we need to adapt to the exponential growth of technology to help students become information and digital literate. Every person must be prepared for the new world economy that is driven by the increase of automation and digitization, and develop their skill sets as jobs continue to be reshaped. To that end, our education system must link the learning in the classroom to the ever changing world of work. Our failure to prepare students and adults by adapting to this dramatic infusion of automation at every level of our work will result in lost jobs if our nation does not act.

Adults who work in the system where their jobs can easily be automated or digitized need to take ownership, and recognize that in order to survive they will need to learn new skills to adapt in a changing workforce. This desired outcome requires a major shift in our mindset as well as new policies at all national, state, and local levels. Our employers and business are seeking employees with new skill sets for a changing economy to close the skills gap. The future of jobs, our economy, our prosperity, our ability to become a united society depend on our educational system to transform the way we prepare our next generation workforce. A fundamental principle of the success or failure of a student achieving an aspiring career should not be based on where student live or their zip code. To achieve this democratic right, our school system needs to be redesigned into a new learning system to provide a quality educational experience that impacts the 21st Century learner.

A New Learning System

The learning system has evolved to transition from a time where students were expected to be in a physical place to learn, to a time where the learning comes to the students. From the initial single schoolhouse setting until most recently, students had to physically attend a classroom or a place to learn where a teacher engages students with the curriculum content. With the breakthrough of digital media, the internet and online learning platforms, students and adults can learn from anywhere, at any time, at any pace using any platform based on their convenient schedule and learning style.

> The more technology advances the more the learning and education system must adapt to leverage technology to support student learning in the K-12 system.

Online and cloud-based platforms are playing an important role in augmenting learning for students as well as professional adult learners. At the same time, the role of the teacher has dramatically transitioned from a teacher-centered delivery of content to the role of a student-centered facilitator of learning. Access to content on the Internet and other digital resources has and will continue to transform the way we all learn. It is clear and important to state that technology will not replace the teacher in the classroom, but rather the teacher's role in guiding and shaping the learning experience. The challenge for our teachers and administrators is to design a learning system whereby technology may assist, guide, and shape the learning process based on each students learning goals.

As technology continues to accelerate the structure of the learning system, constant advancement in the learning modalities such as mobile technology, artificial intelligence, virtual reality and machine learning will continue to impact everyone. One true axiom is that the more technology advances the more the learning and education system must adapt to leverage technology to support student learning in the K-12 system. The greatest challenges education and those who work in the system face is their ability to learn new practices and unlearn old practices while developing new strategies for teaching and learning.

> When students are exposed to ubiquitous technology in their personal lives they will expect at least the same level of technology integration within their learning activities, both inside and outside the classroom.

As the rate of innovation accelerates with new products and resources emerge, there becomes an increasing demand for professional learning for all teachers and administrators. When students are exposed to ubiquitous technology in their personal lives they will expect at least the same level of technology integration within their learning activities, both inside and outside the classroom. One thing is certain—the cell phone and tech tools students are holding in their hands will be the worst technology they will possess in their lifetime.

Students moving through the educational system are exposed to learning technology at various levels of sophistication. Unfortunately, there is an equity issue as not all students at all schools have the same level of access to technology. There are various reasons for this unleveled playing field due primarily to the lack of vision or understanding for how to integrate technology, including the economic and budgetary crises in education. A major inhibitor is the lack of adequate professional learning to help prepare teachers who have yet to become accustomed to implementing instructional technology in the classroom. However, there are a number of innovative and creative teachers who are taking charge of their professional learning setting the trend, and modeling for their colleagues the effective use of technology integration. We need these teachers to function as "Learning Design Coaches", and support their teacher colleagues to transform the classroom of the future.

The argument whether technology is effective or not, and whether it should be incorporated in the classroom is no longer in dispute. One only needs to look at how most young and even adults are obsessed with the use of their cell phones and unwillingness to live without their phones in a connected world. One of the best ways to integrate technology is to involve students in the learning process, and have students showcase how they use technology to solve problems. When students are involved in the learning process, they become engaged, and can help teachers learn new skills. The question really lies with the appropriate use technology for teaching and learning and not whether technology should be integrated with learning.

What Does It Mean to Be Educated in the 21st Century?

An essential question to explore in our educational system is "What does it mean to be educated in the 21st Century?" We have now lived for almost one-fifth of the 21st Century, and we are still trying to define what students need to learn and be able to do. The State Standards have been developed to provide guidance as to what students should learn, yet they do not define how teachers should teach and design the learning environment for students. Teachers have and should be given the autonomy to design the learning environment in their classroom. Yet, when many classroom of today still resemble the classroom of the past half-century then there is a need to pull the fire alarm.

Our world and our knowledge-sharing economy is not the same, and neither should the classroom of tomorrow be. The secret sauce is to design a system where students have what is coined as "Voice and Choice" of their learning. Students must take ownership of their learning and learn how to learn, how to assess their own progress. Alan November in his book, *Who Owns the Learning,* in the chapter "Age of the Empowered Learner" states that we must have students take responsibility to manage their learning. John Hattie, another well-known author, has conducted a meta-analysis on effective teaching practices. He has provided guidance to the student learner as they learn to assess their own learning with three essential questions: "Where am I at?", "Where am I going?", and "What's Next?" These are foundation for Student Agency as students learn to control and manage their own learning. Developing these skills is paramount in the age of student-centric learning so they may understand how to navigate through the information overload, social media, and alternative news sources.

Many organizations such as International Society for Technology in Educations (ISTE) (iste.org), CUE (cue.org), Consortium for School Networking (CoSN) (cosn.org), Technology Information Center for Administrative Leadership (TICAL) (portical.org), and California Educational Technology Professionals Association (CETPA) (cetpa.net) have developed standards and guidelines for how to effectively implement instructional technology in the classroom. In addition, the Digital Promise (http://digitalpromise.org) created a system to accelerate digital innovation in education. They have also developed the League of Innovative Schools, a consortium of superintendent leaders who push the innovation in their districts by sharing their best and next practices. There are a number of webinars and blogs, too many to name, that outline strategies and best practices for effective implementation of instructional technologies. An emerging theme from these organizations is to promote personalization of learning and innovation in the classroom. Unfortunately, schools need to catch up and keep up with the acceleration of change in the workforce. So why can't we move the needle fast enough to engage all our teachers and all our students?

A Shift from No Child Left Behind Act to Every Student Succeeds Act

The underlying issue is the education system itself is not functioning at optimum effectiveness, and many would argue it needs to be redesigned differently. The problem is systemic in nature, and the system itself must continue to evolve. It requires leadership at all levels of the organization starting with Boards of Education and Superintendents, including staff and community in the change process. Our system is not moving fast enough, and the longer we wait the more students we leave ill-prepared for a rapidly changing workforce. Our workers continue to see jobs moving oversees and to other countries with lower wages. The result in the past is a whole generation of workers who were laid off due to the advancement of automation, digitalization, computerization, and the changing dynamics of the work. If workers are unable to retool their skills, then we have a major economic and social dilemma that keeps escalating. Unfortunately, the old jobs have gone away and will not return in the same form. The only choice for our students, including ALL adults, young and old, is to prepare themselves for a new technologically-advanced workforce or risk losing their jobs.

The concerns stretch back to the "Nation at Risk" report in the mid 1980's to the movement of the No Child Left Behind Act (NCLB) in 2002. The NCLB mandate has left an imprint on our system and society no matter your view point. How can anyone argue with the concept of not leaving a child behind? Although the concept had merit, it resulted in an accountability system designed to measure student outcomes focused more on content mastery and test-taking skills rather than place a value on thinking skills and competency based skills. Essentially, knowing the correct answer was more important than how you got the correct solution. Unfortunately, in the real world it doesn't work that way. In business and other professions there is rarely one right answer. Often in business and the real world, the correct answer is based on various daily conditions and environment of the day which may change the next day based on circumstances. When hiring, business doesn't care *what you know, it's what you do with what you know.* So how do we design an educational system that links the learning in the classroom to the real-world application of knowledge in both predictable and unpredictable settings?

Rigor, Relevance, Relationships

Twenty five years ago Dr. Bill Daggett, the President of the International Center of Leadership and Education, designed a Rigor and Relevance Framework that addressed the need to focus more on higher order thinking. The Rigor and Relevance Framework later included the Relationship component. Dr. Daggett espoused that student experiences need to focus less on rote memory (Quadrant A: Acquisition of knowledge) where students were passive learners, and the teacher did most of the talking and work. Rather, students need to solve complex problems (Quadrant D: Adaptation) where they did most of the thinking and work. It was not good enough to know the answer but how to apply complex thinking and problem solving skills in both predictable and unpredictable real world settings. This model design is consistent with the educational standards across the nation aligned to promote the Common Core which was sponsored by the National Governors Association (NGA) and the Council of Chief State School Officers (CCSSO).

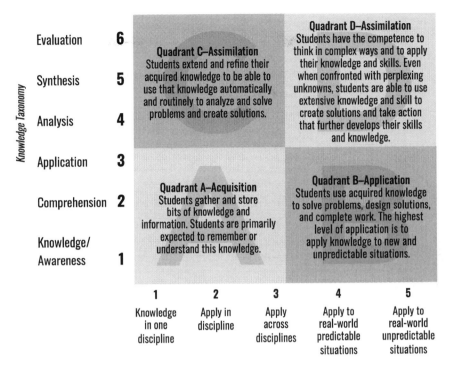

Figure 1-3. Application Model

While many states implemented the Common Core, some states received push back from the political arena because it was viewed as a national reform agenda. Several critics took opposition to the Common Core as a national movement to centralize our education system. Yet, it was not understood that all states are required to adopt their own content standards under their local control. Many of the states in doing so disassociated themselves with the "Common Core" term, and simply referred to their curriculum content at the "State Standard". Nevertheless, the concept of the new State Standards was designed to be aligned with grade level Language Arts and Math standards. Many states have also adopted new technology adaptive assessments administered on a computer or mobile devices with a specific browser that maintained security provisions.

An education mantra has been "What gets measured gets taught." If the education system is designed to hold our students, teachers, and administrators accountable for what students need to know and be able to do, then the new State Standards and new assessment system needed to be in alignment. As we have learned from previous implementation of new standards and assessments, it generally takes five years or more to have teachers and the system catch up. Yet, the current challenges are more complex, and it is not so much the content and assessment itself, rather the use of an online assessment system. This new format requires students to use technology with complex structure for responding to the performance tasks.

Many in education, including Board members who adopt policy, and allocate funds for technology, as they began to recognize that students were required to take the online technology assessment to demonstrate competency, recognized that education needed to invest heavily in the accountability system. It could be argued that if students know the standards, but lacked the technology skills to demonstrate the appropriate response, the results may lead to a potentially low assessment scores. This notion to the Board members and Superintendents was an alarming wake-up call that pushed the need for teacher professional learning and upgrading the technology network and deployment of computers/laptops for students. It is evident that simply providing technology in the classroom is not the solution in and of itself...it is more complex.

College, Career, and Life Ready

Concurrently, a movement focused and began to shift from the traditional College Readiness to College and Career Readiness. This shift occurred prior the NCLB legislation was to sunset, as more and more schools were not able to meet the 100 percent accountability compliance by 2014. The Every Student Succeeds Act (ESSA) signed into law by President Obama in December 2015 emerged with a focus on college and career readiness. In fact, many districts included "Life Readiness" as a major component when a greater emphasis was placed on the Social Emotional Learning as a necessary component of students graduating from high school. College, Career, and Life Readiness goes beyond the basic one size fits all skills and expanded to prepare students for the real world of work. Students graduating from high school need Career Technical Education (CTE) in conjunction with meeting the A-G College readiness requirements.

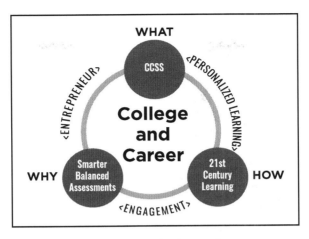

Figure 1-2. Linked Learning

Linked Learning

College, Career, and Life Readiness is designed to prepare students for a rapidly changing world. Linking the learning in the classroom to real world settings requires teachers to develop complex strategies. Many concepts such as deeper learning, project-based learning, competency-based learning, and personalized learning have arisen to support the Digital Learning Transformation movement. The challenge for many teachers is to design a learning environment that connects all these essential components into a cohesive learning structure. This is hard work and a heavy lift for our teachers and education system, not to mention how technology is to be incorporated into the mix.

The Figure 1.2 serves to link the essential components as a way to explain how the new system could be redesigned. The new State Standards define "What" students need to learn and be able to do; integrate 21st Century Learning strategies for "How" to learn; the new online assessment systems measures the "Why" students should apply the learning; collectively the model demonstrates the graduate profile for college and career. In this model, personalized learning is the driver from the "What" to the "How"; engagement with the 21st Century Learning strategies through the application of knowledge demonstrates the competency from the "How" to the "Why"; developing an entrepreneurship skill sets becomes the basis for a student to demonstrate they are ready for the "What" of their aspiration to be college and career ready.

Organizations Supporting the System Redesign

The Linked Learning Alliance (linkedlearning.org) with the support of the James Irvine Foundation has led the movement and policy implication for designing a system to promote real thinking and problem solving skills. "The Linked Learning Approach integrates rigorous academics that meet college-ready standards with sequenced, high-quality career-technical education, work-based learning, and supports to help students stay on track." [1]

The Partnership for 21st Century Learning (p21.org) under the leadership of David Ross, Executive Director, is another organization since the '90s that has promoted the 21st Century Skills of the 4 Cs: critical thinking, creativity, communication, and collaboration. Recently, schools have added addition Cs such as character, competency and civility to the 21st Century skills. These are the fundamental skills that employers are looking for when hiring students and adults with the necessary skills to be an effective knowledge worker.

The National Academy Foundation (NAF), based in New York, under the leadership of President JD Hoye has developed a partnership with business and major corporate entities who understand the need to design interdisciplinary academies that provide a strong work-based program that includes job shadowing and internships. With the support of a strong school to business partnership the NAF has grown to over 750 academies predominantly at the high school level to prepare students for both college and career. More importantly, students who typically are low performing and disengaged begin to develop a sense of personal pride and commitment to a strong academy model aligned with a career pathway.

The Buck Institute is one of the premiere models that promote project-based learning (PBL). Schools throughout the nation are incorporating PBL as an instructional strategy to actively engage students to solve complex problem by beginning with the end in mind. Students are exposed to real world problem, and learn how to manage projects with design and assessments elements incorporated into their project.

---

[1] http://www.linkedlearning.org/about/

"Project-based learning is a teaching method in which students gain knowledge and skills by working for an extended period of time to investigate and respond to an authentic, engaging, and complex question, problem, or challenge." [2]

Digital Learning Transformation

The roadmap for a successful digital learning transformation begins with a strong vision that defines and articulates how all the complex systems are connected. Often, when I speak with educators, their measure of success for being technology-driven is their ability to provide students with devices. It seems like everyone's priority in education is to become a 1:1 district with ubiquitous access to technology and Internet connectivity both at school and home. At the same time, we hear it is "not about the technology", but rather about the teaching and learning processes that transform our students as 21st century learners. In fact, too much emphasis is placed on which device to purchase when the conversation should be device agnostic. The planning of a strong technology design should start with the technology infrastructure, bandwidth connectivity, and network system based on the desired student learning environment. Living in this panacea that technology itself will transform our students as 21st century learners is not a good argument. Although there is a major shift toward digital transformation and innovation in our schools, administrators need to understand how to connect the dots and develop a comprehensive implementation plan that impacts student learning. The plan needs to go beyond the technology infrastructure and include a comprehensive professional learning, technology refresh plan, and model for effective teaching and learning.

Future Ready

The Alliance of Excellence in Education led by the former Governor of West Virginia, Bob Wise, coordinated an effort with the White House and the U.S. Department of Education Office of Ed Technology, to create the Future Ready initiative. This initiative was designed to draw the attention to school district superintendents and the need for a digital transformation. In November 2014, President Obama brought to the

---

[2] http://www.bie.org/about

Figure 1-3. FRS Framework

White House over 100 superintendents to take a pledge, and commit to supporting students to prepare them with digital skills and resources necessary to excel in the 21st century. In an effort to expand access to high-speed internet in school President Obama stated, "In a country where we expect free Wi-Fi with our coffee, we should definitely demand it in our schools." [3]

A good place to begin the process can be found at www. FutureReady.org. First, the district superintendent must take the Future Ready pledge to qualify and commit to the Future Ready project. Taking the Future Ready assessment collectively with your team validates different viewpoints that the district is headed in the right direction. There is a comprehensive five-step process that outlines how to gather and interpret the data. Review the report as a team, then move your efforts to the next level by taking advantage of the resources available at the Future Ready Hub.

This collaborative process of taking the Future Ready assessment provides a professional learning opportunity to build innovative

---

[3] https://obamawhitehouse.archives.gov/the-press-office/2014/02/remarks-president-connected

leadership capacity within your team. The leadership team will benefit from this process, and understand the major implementation shifts and design elements for the appropriate technology solutions. Through the assessment dashboard, the leadership team will discover where it is on the continuum for the digital conversion, identify gaps, access strategies, and review its progress toward the development of a robust technical and human infrastructure. An essential step is to develop an Action Plan, and examine best practice strategies from other districts to build into the Innovation Plan.

What innovative leaders will learn from this process is the need to move beyond thinking about 21st Century learning skills as technology-based and focus instead on creating a personalized learning environment which prepares students for college, career, and life readiness. Linking the learning in the classroom to a real world setting makes the learning relevant, and brings life to the curriculum so that students are engaged and feel connected to their future career path.

Personalized Learning to an Entrepreneur Mindset

As mentioned previously, one concept is to design a personalized learning model that builds on the learning outcomes to develop students as entrepreneurs. This does not imply that students must start their own business; yet, it does require students to develop an "entrepreneurial mindset" where they can think, act, feel, and behave like an entrepreneur. Millennial students are wired to develop these creative skills sets when they are young. Providing learning opportunities around project-based activities and designing strategies as if they are starting their own business prepares them to think like an entrepreneur.

We can make learning relevant by creating a learning environment in schools where student design a real life problem they wish to solve and design a project to solve that problem. How exciting would that be! Imagine the answer to the question "What did you do in school today?" where what students did in school has a real connection to problems they see in the world and their ability to solve them.

A true entrepreneur is able to identify a real world problem, and fill the gap by designing a solution to meet the needs of society. Wouldn't going to school be more fun, engaging, and relevant if students could do this too? We often hear the stories about a college dropout who ends up becoming a great entrepreneur by designing a product that we all want to buy. So why can't our students start learning as early as elementary school to come up with similar solutions? They can; we—the adults—just need to help change the system to allow our students to become creative innovators, and release the power of their entrepreneur mindset. Students have the capacity to actually design a project, or better yet, create a solution to solve a hairy, audacious problem that people deal with every day. We just need to give them the time, resources, tools, coaching, and permission to step out of their comfort zone.

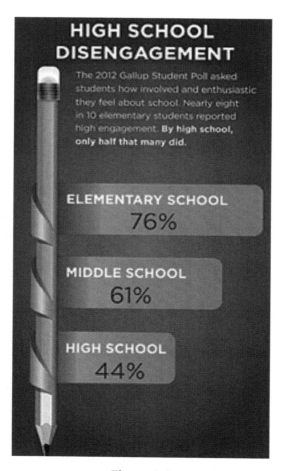

Figure 1-4

Student Engagement

The Gallup poll study demonstrates the level of student engagement as they move from elementary school to middle school to high school. The study reports that 76 percent of elementary students are engaged, 61 percent of middle school students, and dropping down to 44 percent of high school students are engaged. This negative engagement trend indicates that as students get older, they tend to be less engaged.[4]

Although there may be a number of reasons, an argument could be made that elementary students typically have one teacher who holds a multiple subject credential that supports the students most of the day. The elementary teacher also has fewer students to support, allowing him or her to develop a strong relationship with students. Conversely, the middle and high school students typically have multiple teachers in their daily schedule who hold a single subject credential for their specialized field. The secondary teacher at the middle school or high could have as many as 175 students for their five-period teaching day. It is certainly a challenge to build a relationship with a large student-teacher ratio, and in many cases the challenge of personalizing the learning experience is daunting.

Given the current conditions in our education system, the challenge is to examine how to appropriately use and leverage technology while incorporating project-based learning as well as deeper learning to fully engage students no matter their grade level. When students are fully engaged and connected to their learning with an adult both inside and outside the classroom, then there is a greater likelihood that they will achieve at a high level.

So now is the time to go beyond the 1:1 devices and technology integration, and change the learning system to create entrepreneurial students who graduate with the skills for college, career and life. We may just engage students in their learning and witness less discipline problems, fewer suspensions, a lower dropout rate, and a higher graduation rate. Sounds like this may even address your district's Local Control Accountability Plan goals in California and the Every Student Succeed Act (ESSA) guidelines!

---

[4] http://www.gallup.com/services/189926/student-poll-2015-results.aspx

Building Leadership Capacity

As we prepare the next generation of learners, we must also develop the next generation of teachers and administrators. Leadership does matter, and we know that superintendents and Cabinet members must work with their staff to *redesign the learning experience in the digital age.* The digital learning transformation is complex and has multiple components to prepare our students for the knowledge-sharing economy.

So, where do we begin? I can't overemphasize that it all starts with professional learning and building leadership capacity at all levels of the educational system. Dr. David Verdugo, Executive Director for the California Association of Latino Superintendents and Administrators (CALSA) states, "At no other point in time in the field of educational leadership has it been more important to build, persuade, and promote a new set of leaders directly associated with technology, innovation, and school district leadership." [5]

There are number of educational organizations that support technology education professional learning including the Technology Information Center for Administrative Leadership (TICAL—www.portical.org). TICAL is a group of dedicated administrators who designed a learning platform for administrators by administrators. They initiated an annual LEAD3 conference (lead3.org) along with CUE and Association of California School Administrators (ACSA) to focus on sharing best practices for administrators leading educational technology.

These system changes demand and call for a highly skillful superintendent and cabinet to understand the complex technology solutions to be implemented. Building innovative leadership capacity with digital age decision making skills is your ticket to becoming an effective leader at all levels of the organization.

---

[5] http://www.educationinnovationalliance.org/

DR. GABE SOUMAKIAN *is a retired Superintendent who is passionate about supporting school districts through the digital learning transformation to prepare students for College, Career, and Life readiness. For his leadership and innovation in redesigning the high school experience, he was selected as a member of the Digital Promise League of Innovative Schools. He has been actively involved and presented at numerous leadership organizations at the state and national level on Personalized Digital Learning and Linked Learning Academies.*

Dr. Soumakian has served on the Future Ready panel of visionary educators, and has served on the National Academy Foundation Leadership Fellow. He was recognized as one of ten Superintendents nationally for the Lexington Education Leadership Award (LELA) Fellow in conjunction with EdElements. Since 2000, he has served as a cadre member of the Technology Information Center for Administrative Leadership (TICAL) that supports districts through the educational technology. Dr. Soumakian has over 35 years of education experience, including 18 years as a high school teacher.

2

The Promise and Challenge of Technology in K-12 Education—Setting the Stage

Dr. Alan R. Shark

By the time a youngster enters kindergarten he or she has most likely been exposed to the use of technologies in ways teachers and administrators had never experienced. On average, children are getting their first smartphone by the age of ten, and the downward trend continues.[1] Seventy-two percent of children under the age of eight have used a smart device for media consumption such as watching videos, playing games, or apps.[2] A look at toys sold just five years ago compared to today shows a dramatic change towards technology-driven devices that speak, listen, act, challenge, move, fly, and inform. Some of this can be accomplished by the push of a button or the sound of a voice. What happens when the young enter the classroom for the first time? Will the experience be exhilarating, or might it be boring by lacking a sense of challenge? One does not need to be an educational expert to know that when students get bored or do not properly assimilate into the education system at the earliest ages, the foundational learning blocks that can lead to success can lead to the exact opposite.

[1] https://goo.gl/cPlgec

[2] https://goo.gl/jxGok2

The digital journey through- out K-12 continues to evolve at a dizzying pace albeit unevenly from state to state. Overall, advances in technology are indeed growing exponentially with each new advance quickly building upon the last. Information technology in particular serves as a powerful enabler that empowers people in ways that few could have contemplated just a few short years ago. Each one awakes to rather staggering future predictions regarding technology, such as Internet traffic will pass the zettabyte range by the year 2018, and also by 2018, global Internet traffic will be 64 times the entire volume of the Internet in 2005. Similarly, by 2018, the gigabyte equivalent of all movies ever made will cross the Internet every three minutes.[3] Such examples are becoming as ubiquitous as they are impossible to visualize. If anyone needed convincing that the *Internet of Everything* had arrived, 2013 was the year when we realized that there were more mobile devices in the U.S. than people. Data communications surpassed voice, and machines are talking to one another almost as much as humans talk to one another. Clearly, the Internet of Everything is now, even though it is still growing in size and scope. No institution, especially K-12 can escape its grasp. Some will view current events with fear and worry, while others will marvel about the possibilities and opportunities.

> 2013 was the year when we realized that there were more mobile devices in the U.S. than people.

The digital journey in K-12 education encompasses connected knowledge, new learning tools for teachers and students, increased mobility, enhanced information technology (IT) infrastructure that includes desktop virtualization and unified computing systems, and finally, virtual and connected classrooms.

What follows is a quick tour that further highlights some of the key trends impacting K-12 education.

The Smart Classroom

With the rapidly expanding use and impact of technology by today's young students, the actual physical classroom has evolved—with more

---

[3]http://www.cisco.com/web/about/ac79/docs/IoE/IoE-VAS_Public-Sector_Top-10-Insights.pdf

displays and less structured seating aimed at encouraging collaboration and perhaps the fun of leaning through exploring. Schools have begun replacing furniture, and are looking at specialized lighting that can simulate sunlight, as well as adjust to the time of day or learning environment. Chairs that were one bolted to the floor are now on wheels that can be adjusted for comfort, and in some cases can provide storage underneath the chair.

Many traditional classrooms have been converted into multi-media rooms, where giant video screens adorn the walls. Some rooms are equipped with one or more large screens, some equipped with special writing devices that allow teachers to draw over any screen display or simply write notes or post questions. In other words, this relatively new option is like having a digital whiteboard for all to see, share, and perhaps save for future reference. This same smart-room technology provides the option of having students display what is on their own mobile devices. A student can share a presentation or even a website without leaving his or her seat.

To encourage greater student interaction and participation, student response systems are used. For example, instead of or in addition to one raising one's hand for recognition, all students can be asked to respond to a question using a handheld device referred to as a student response system or simply a "clicker." The student can click off what he or she thinks via polling or responding to a particular question, be it yes or no or multiple choice. The main advantage using such

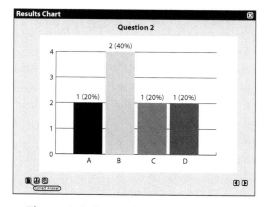

Figure 2-1. Sample of a digital clicker

Figure 2-2. Example of clicker results

devices is that it allows for 100 percent participation and interaction, where results are often displayed on a large screen, where instant results can be viewed by all to see, and where teachers can identify challenges students are having and respond immediately, rather than waiting for the results of a paper and pen test or quiz.

The Personal Screen

While personal computer sales are at record lows, the sale of netbooks and tablets is sky-high. It is the ultra-low cost and functionality that make this device a winner in the K-12 market. As long as there is ample and reliable broadband coupled with a strong central network, having "thin client" devices with a brilliant screen, good battery life, and a wireless adapter is all that is needed to bring the wealth of the connected world into the hands of students. Each unit can be configured or virtualized to what the student needs, and instead of having everything stored on each unit, data is stored on the network where it is safer and more manageable. Tablets can be configured similarly thus saving school districts thousands if not millions of dollars in unneeded hardware. Today's devices are smaller, lighter, and more portable than ever, thus meeting the needs of a mobile environment where a student can bring his or device from class to class. Some school districts have experimented with bring your own device (BYOD) programs which can be quite beneficial for those with the means to bring their own devices to school, but may run into issues of equity regarding those who can't afford to purchase their own devices.

And while small screen devices are excellent for individual learning, other technologies are superior at engaging groups and encouraging collaboration. We know that machines alone are limited without good content.

When it comes to content one naturally turns to the Internet. And the Internet of Things (IoE) has become an accepted term that describes how our society has become so interconnected both nationally and globally. Students sitting in a classroom in Brooklyn, New York can view live video feeds from all over the nation, which might include guest teachers or subject matter experts in another city or country. This is another way of saying that technology can bring data and information to life! Thousands of video cameras are in active use throughout cities, zoos, nature preserves, and museums. They can provide free access to view what's going on day or night to just about anyone with a smart device or computer. Someone in Chicago can watch a live feed of panda bears at the Smithsonian National Zoo in Washington, D. C. or the birth of a baby eagle braking through its shell in Oregon. This is but another way we can all be observers of life as it unfolds, and yet, still be able to provide and share content.

YouTube has emerged as the video touchpoint of life for millions of people—300 hours of video, coming from 71 countries and in 61 languages are loaded onto YouTube every hour.[4] The point to all this is that there is no longer any shortage of content—indeed there is infinitely more content than a few years ago, but is it accurate, fair, tested, reviewed, and relevant? Here is where we must rely on teachers and instructional designers to help curate.

Social Media Competing for Attention

There is great reluctance among teachers to include social media into the classroom. The reasons given are usually one of trying to keep students focused on the lesson plan and not on what the latest gossip is trending. According to a Pew Research Center study, 24 percent of teens use social media constantly.[5] The report also stated that Facebook was the most popular and frequently used social media platform among

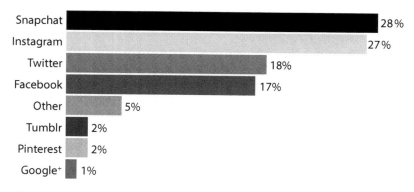

Figure 2-3. Use of social media by teens, 2016 (SOURCE: FORTUNE.COM)

---

[4] http://www.youtube.com/yt/press/statistics.html

[5] http://www.pewinternet.org/2015/04/09/teens-social-media-technology-2015/

teens; half of teens use Instagram, and nearly as many use Snapchat. However, a year later a more recent study reported in Fortune showed that teens in the Spring of 2016 greatly preferred Snapchat, Instagram, and Twitter greatly over Facebook.[6]

Reasons given tend to vary, but most teens tend to agree it is the simplicity and immediateness that makes taking pictures and adding captions a great way to connect with friends.

Educators have a real challenge, and some say an opportunity, when it comes to social media. While social media can (and do) compete for attention when it comes to formalized learning, they can also be included in many course topics. For example, social media can be used to better illustrate the need for good "digital hygiene" and "digital ethics" when it comes to what can be shared and what *should* be shared. Students need to understand the risks. Discussions might revolve around cautioning about the effects of cyberbullying or basic safety in not revealing too much personal information, as well as the need to understand the consequences in a world where nothing really gets erased. Social media can be used to explore issues in greater depth and learn how to be better critics of news and information through better understanding of sources.

Rise of E-Books

E-book sales peaked in 2013, and have declined or held steady since then. Disadvantages include the inability to share, donate, or resell "used" materials. Another disadvantage is that e-book pricing remains rather close to printed materials. The advantages of e-books include the fact that they can be tied to active media references that allow students to click on locations on maps, immediate links to definitions, references, and pop-up video clips that further illustrate learning. Another advantage is that e-books allow for quicker fact updates and additions which are especially helpful and critical in an ever-changing world. E-books still show growth in the next decade.

Transmedia Enhancement

Great devices are only effective if they are used to their advantage, and that translates into meaningful content. Rather than simply watch a

---

[6] http://fortune.com/2016/04/13/snapchat-instagram-piper-jaffray/

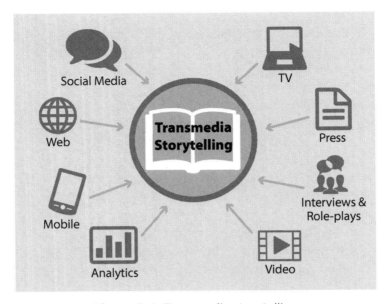

Figure 2-4. Transmedia storytelling

topical video, many have found ways to make the video experience more interactive. One key example is story telling. Storytelling, a centuries-old method of communication, is greatly enhanced by the various forms of media. We now find terms such as "transmedia" or "multimode" that take storytelling to new levels by utilizing various media platforms that can switch between video presentations, audio, games, pictures, charts, etc. Schools spend more than $3,000,000,000 per year on digital content.[7]

Wi-Fi Expansion

The physical structures of our nation's schools haven't changed much over time until recently. Some of the changes are visible, while others are not something one can see. In 2008, many schools banned Wi-Fi access in hallways, classrooms, and school yards. Wireless connections to the Internet was viewed as a distraction or an intrusion because students could text or surf the web while in class, and thus pay little attention to what was going on in classroom. Schools are beginning to open up their wireless space for students and teachers at the K-12 level.

---

[7] http://www.edweek.org/ew/issues/technology-in-education/

While most schools created "no Wi-Fi" or "no mobile device" zones, the trend now appears to be moving in the opposite direction. Today, we are seeing a whole new generation of expanded and more powerful Wi-Fi options throughout schools. Many teachers now encourage students to search the Internet for certain things as part of class instruction and include such activity as part of class participation and interaction.

Connected Learning

Schools are using technology to bring in expertise and subject matter to supplement what may be unavailable at any particular school or location. A teacher at a remote location with a particular specialty can broadcast to a class thousands of miles away. Similarly, students, who may be homebound due to illness or weather, may join a class from just about anywhere. Connected learning enables greater individual leaning, and can focus on a particular student's need or interest. Connected learning recognizes that "one size may not fit all," and this is where technology can serve as an enabler through on-demand individualized learning. Massachusetts Institute of Technology's Office of Digital learning says it best, "Digital learning technologies can enable students to grasp concepts more quickly and fully, to connect theory and application more adeptly, and to engage in learning more readily, while also improving instructional techniques, leveraging instructor time, and facilitating the widespread sharing of knowledge. Digital technologies

Figure 2-5

will enable this in new and better ways, and create possibilities beyond the limits of our current imagination." [8]

Cloud-Based Solutions

Cloud-based solutions are perhaps one of the greatest game-changers when it comes to technology and, in particular, education. Demands for faster network speeds, greater storage and the growth of apps have placed a lot of demand on school system networks—be it stand-alone or part of a larger network. Cloud-based solutions provide many significant advantages over having to maintain everything in one physical location. This shift from owning and operating to managing and coordinating enables schools to contract for the type and amount of technology to be operated (either hardware and/or software applications) as well as the amount actually used. The burden of always keeping up with technology improvements, updates, security patches, as well as refreshed and updated equipment, becomes the responsibility of the cloud provider. In other words, the cloud model today is moving from a tech-centric environment to one that is service-centric.

> The cloud model today is moving from a tech-centric environment to one that is service-centric.

The benefits of utilizing cloud-based solutions go far beyond network efficiencies, as it provides the opportunity for greater ease of access, collaboration, and mobility. Cloud-based solutions almost always lead to simpler user interfaces that can be accessed on almost any authorized device and just about anywhere there is broadband connectivity—wired or wireless.

Instructional and Video Support

Similar to connected learning, instructional and video support can lead toward improved teacher effectiveness and student learning. While many schools possess the latest in video equipment, they all too often fall short in providing the necessary staff support. It is not unusual for teachers to complain that they would be more inclined to utilize

---

[8] https://odl.mit.edu/value-digital-learning

technology in the classroom if they had more help in understanding and learning to operationalize best practices and how to use the various hardware and software offerings. It is somewhat ironic that the one of the main weaknesses in technology in the K-12 environment is the lack of leadership in insisting on, and thus proving a true technology support system for teachers and students.

Thanks to improvements and the growth of broadband, asynchronous online learning systems have greatly improved. Students can untether themselves from an office phone or speaker phone, and listen to a class or an instructor's lecture. Today's technology permits students to use their tablets to both see and hear their online classmates and instructors. They can view online assignments, ask questions, view videos and readings, and track their progress at any time. Telepresence technology allows participants at various locations to see and hear one another as if they were in the same location in one another's virtual presence. This technology is excellent for learning, interviewing guests, or visiting experts and speakers. Video platforms like WebEx, Telepresence, Go-To-Meetings, Adobe Connect, Polycom, LifeSize etc. are just a few of the more popular video services and platforms used by higher education. Some of the platforms are web-based thus allowing for viewing multi-media, PowerPoint presentations, and live or recorded classes offered in high-definition video and sound. Using mobile devices such as tablets, students can conduct and record interviews, check out environmental issues in the field, conduct surveys, and do other forms of research. Sensors that are tapped into the Internet of Everything can be used to gather and share data.

Students can be almost anywhere using their mobile devices to access digital libraries and references located in their home or school or even the Library of Congress. The new mobile order is here, where aside from a near insatiable demand for mobile growth, we will see a rise in software platforms and apps as well as newer and faster speeds and capacity.

Online Assessment

Learning requires measurement and assessment in order to ensure learning truly occurs, and student placement is based on data and achievement. Today, online systems keep accurate records from teachers and often provide learning portals for both students and parents.

Usually, the more parental interaction, the greater the student achievement. And if there is a problem, it can often be spotted early—before becoming a crisis. Parents can now receive weekly or bi-weekly progress reports. Instead of teachers merely leaving numeric or letter grades, they have the option of adding a short video critique thus making evaluation and feedback more meaningful and helpful to the student. Such programs are made possible through the use of advanced technologies and learning management systems (LMS). LMSs provide a portal for posting papers, assignments, articles, videos, websites, and other types of content, such as course wikis and student grades. LMSs also authenticate users and serve as a video and multi-media portal that offers almost unlimited resources to students for both learning and remediation.

As LMSs have become more sophisticated, they can measure a student's progress at any time. For example, they can let the teacher know how many times a student and/or parent was online and the duration and frequency of checking in with the class.

Final Thoughts and Future Trends

New technologies will be added to the learning environment that will make learning and experimentation much more exciting and rewarding. One example is the introduction of 3-D printers which have moved quickly from being a novelty invention in search of a market to an estimated $16,000,000,000+ industry by 2018.[9] Once limited to producing plastic jewelry reproductions, the 3-D printer can now produce materials ranging from precious metals to human cartilage to toys and game parts. One amazing example occurred when the International Space Station, in need of a specialized part, was able to produce it about 250 miles above Earth using an onboard 3-D printer that received specifications and instructions that traveled some 17,000 miles per hour to reach it. Students can not only learn about such technologies—they can experience it through creating objects too.

Today, 3-D printer models are available from retail outlets such as Office Depot, Amazon, and Best Buy. This type of device can be an excellent way of creating and duplicating objects relating to industrial

---

[9] http://www.forbes.com/sites/louiscolumbus/2014/08/09/roundup-of-3d-printing-market-forecasts-and-estimates-2014/

Figure 2-10. 3-D printer

design, especially transportation, printed organs in the medical field, industrial and consumer product-prototype design, environmental design, especially wind-driven power devices and solar-power panel design. 3-D printers allow students to experience hands-on design without having to travel to an industrial lab that could be hundreds, if not thousands, of miles away. This technology provides the opportunity to experiment with exotic materials and new designs.

The next breakthrough in technology that also can enhance learning experiences will come in the form of wearable devices. Examples are smart glasses and visual headsets. Google Glass was considered a breakthrough when it first appeared in 2013 as a hands-free device that provided key information from a mobile device to a special eyepiece. After much publicity, it was shelved in 2015 for further development.

While Google Glass may be back in the planning stages, other companies, such as HTOC's Vive and Microsoft, promise to address the need to better visualize objects and data. HoloLens is designed to work with the new and more powerful desktop computers that will provide augmented-reality applications.[10] This device will be different in that the user can read data right on the lens, experience virtual reality and immersive sounds. The units contain a host of sensors that track one's every move so that as you turn your head, your field of view changes accordingly. The main advantage of this technology is applied augmented reality. Augmented reality allows a user to see maps,

---

[10] http://www.polygon.com/2015/1/21/7867641/windows-holographic-is-the-next-era-of-windows

pictures, and diagrams while also having visual data superimposed. Once commercially available, students and faculty will be able to see, share, and explore things as never before.[11]

Perhaps the newest advances are appearing in the field of robotics and in particular robots. Robots are being introduced as an enhanced learning tool as well as a means to bring in students remotely and subject matter experts as if they were in the room.

Outside of the classroom, technologies are playing an increasingly important role. For example, geographic information systems are used to plan the best school bus routes based on schedules and student addresses. Using vehicle tracking technologies, administrators and parents alike can see where their children's school bus is located on a map using a mobile app or going online. School perimeter and internal cameras now track the school perimeter and hallways for safety enhancement. Smart buildings help control costs by better monitoring of energy usage in regards to lighting as well as cooling and heating. Facility usage including sporting events can be better scheduled and managed through facilities management and reservations systems. The digital journey in the K-12 environment is evolutionary and moving quickly. The learning environment will forever be changed by the many advances in technology as the class of 2020 will surely enjoy many exciting opportunities to learn, experience, and create.

The future for technology for K-12 is bright and filled with many opportunities, and while we search for greater opportunities, there are some key questions that need to be asked, such as:

- To what extent is innovation and technology encouraged and rewarded for teachers?
- To what extent do state curriculum standards encourage the use of technology and learning?
- How much attention is paid toward IT Governance?
- How effective is your technology strategic planning process?
- How much training and support is offered to teachers and staff?
- Is information technology viewed as an investment or merely an expense?

---

[11] http://www.forbes.com/sites/insertcoin/2015/01/25/could-microsofts-hololens-be-the-real-deal/

- How can the case for greater use of technology be rationalized to policy-makers and public managers?
- How can we make sure that children do not embrace technology to the detriment of human contact and understanding?
- What policies and procedures are in place to guard against, prevent, and punish cyber-bullying?
- How do we better ensure digital equity when it comes to income disparity among students?
- How do we promote the need for greater digital literacy and responsibility when it involves copyright, the temptation to sourcing content and guarding against plagiarism?

The K-12 experience is paramount for creating a solid foundation in regards to learning, thinking, socializing, and knowledge. Education leaders, teachers and parents alike must recognize two major things. First, technology is simply a set of tools that if used properly can lead to positive and measured results. And second, it takes a number of key actors to make innovation work that includes but is not limited to the superintendent, principal teacher, Chief Information Officer, and perhaps parents. Innovation requires vision, commitment, and leadership. Innovation in technology in education is like a growing tidal wave, and the challenge is to stay on top, and take advantage of these technologies to improve education.

DR. ALAN R. SHARK *is the Executive Director and CEO of Public Technology Institute (PTI). Dr. Shark is a noted thought-leader, author, and sought-after speaker focusing on mobile and e-government, technology trends in government, as well as thought-leadership professional development issues for IT executives and public managers. Dr. Shark served as editor and contributing author of the book* The Digital Revolution in Higher Education.

He also serves an associate professor of practice at Rutgers University School of Public Affairs & Administration, and is a Fellow of the National Academy of Public Administration where he chairs its Standing Panel on Technology Leadership.

3

The Impact of the Digitization of the Classroom— A Chief Technology Officer's Perspective

Paul Russell

The digitization of the classroom has the potential to provide many great benefits and enhancements to the educational process and learning experience for all involved. The impact of this increased digitized environment has also had a large impact on the technology departments that are required to build, maintain, and support the digitized environments often with the same level of resources or less. Every aspect of the Information Technology (IT) department will need to adapt to the expansion of technologies in the digitized classroom.

> Every aspect of the IT department will need to adapt to the expansion of technologies in the digitized classroom. There will be significant changes in the delivery of services that will impact *staffing, budgeting, and security practices.*

There will be significant changes in the delivery of services that will impact **staffing, budgeting, and security practices.** "Who does what, when, and for how much?" will be a common discussion as the technology use in classrooms increases at a rate greater than we have ever experienced. There will be a need for collaboration, understanding, and empathy for all involved as many of the traditional roles and expectations will shift from traditional to non-traditional IT support. The impact of the digitization can be a great and wonderful learning experience, or it can be a devastating rough ride if not properly planned. This is my story of how the digitization of the classroom became a devastating tsunami of technology. I hope this article enlightens, entertains, but most of all, prepares IT leaders for an exciting and rewarding journey to the digital classroom and to whatever the future holds for us. The Storm has just begun.

The "Good Old Days"

Back on that beautiful calm day all our technologies were performing in perfect harmony because we had "standardized" on a Windows platform with pristine and elegant images for the masses we supported. Caring for a huge number of devices, upwards of 2,000 in all and nearly 1,200 supported customers of technology, we felt confident that everything was well managed and controlled, and our customers loved us as the caregivers and providers of technology. All devices provided to 600 teachers were standard laptops with Wi-Fi enabled, and marching in tune with the IT department's designed images, policies, access, and support. These devices were built on strict, but loving security policies only to protect those unassuming naive natives of technologies. We were there to protect them from themselves and the harms of the outside world—the Internet. These policies and procedures were created with the best, however as misguided as they may have been, intent which may have led to the first wave of this technology tsunami. These naive and unknowing customers of the very technology we provided with such care and preparation wanted more… Imagine more than what we allowed them to have—did I mention they had wireless in all school buildings? The images included security updates every time the computer started and connected to the network that would guarantee safe and secure access to and from the Internet. Yes, these updates may have prevented immediate access to what was needed for the classroom to start, but they are kids, they could find something else to do while these updates occur; after all, it is the security of the network we needed to consider. Once the device was secure and prepared well enough to enter the open waters of the Internet, we then carefully crafted a pathway to only those sites which we in IT knew were appropriate and safe to access for the students and teachers. When a site was not available or blocked, the teacher would "simply" submit a request to the school administration to access to the blocked site. Once the administration reviewed and approved the request, the administration would then send a request to IT to unblock the site. The site was ready for access usually within a week—give or take. Once the site was added to the acceptable sites list, tested, and verified, the teacher would be notified that their request had been approved and granted. The teacher was now able to proceed and go ahead and teach—"What do you mean you don't need it anymore? Why did you ask for us to get this added in the first place? Do you know what it takes to add sites like this constantly?" Learning opportunity—once I heard my staff saying this, it was like I was hit in the face with a wave of reality. I shook my head to clear the cobwebs and said, "Why is it so hard for the teachers to get access to these sites?" and "Why are we the ones deciding if it is ok?" I was too afraid to ask the next question "Did we ever not allow them to access sites they've requested?" I, to this day, hope we never rejected any request. Assuming we in IT never reached that level of audacity, I knew we had to make it easier to let the teachers access the Internet. Teachers were accessing the Internet for educational materials that were not available in the school system, not shopping for deals on e-Bay. We streamlined the process of allowing access to blocked sites to be requested by teachers directly to IT, and prioritized the request to be completed within the day usually within 30 minutes. Yes, this was streamlined compared to the previous process, but still not what the teachers needed. Fully realizing we needed to allow the teachers to add sites as they needed, we replaced the older content filter with an appliance that allows the teacher to register and add the sites as needed, eliminating all delays and interaction with IT unless the site is explicitly block per the Child Internet Protection Act (CIPA) rules.

As I awaited the dedication ceremony, including some sort of parade and a bust of me to be unveiled at the school that would be dedicated in my name for making such a tremendous contribution in the name of education, another wave began to form—the iPad. Surely this consumer-based device that was only for searching the web, taking pictures, and capable of doing some other stuff was not going to be allowed to enter a fine-tuned, well-oiled enterprise network that was created for teachers to access the web with their secured "locked" down computers. There's no way these devices, designed and built by that fruit company, were going to be allowed to enter the pristine, secure Windows environment created for educational use! Was there? I knew these devices could be used to gain access to additional educational materials, and engage students more. Yes, perhaps these devices were becoming much more user friendly—euphemism for "I don't want information technology (IT) to tell me what, where, or how I should teach." What about security? What about access to your Windows-based applications? What about security? Oh, I already said that, but it's important—right? No way these can be easy to use, virus free, educational applications as far as the eye can see. Devices are never going to be used on the windows network—why would you do this? Oh, right, it's for the kids and what they need. Not what IT needs. Learning opportunity number 2. These teachers—they really are educators—look how much I learned so far, and I wasn't even in class—I was getting schooled.

The Warning Signs

When I first heard, "We are thinking we need to bring in newer technologies that will support the educational process and provide a greater learning experience for our students" this was the first sign the storm would be coming. As we learned afterwards, the tsunami that was so devastating to the Philippines, the first indication that many unsophisticated and uneducated but brilliant tribal people observed were animals seeking higher ground—they followed the animals and survived. Those who were more educated, yet less knowledgeable, took a different approach to take in the beauty and experience offered by the receding ocean that left a fresh, clean, and pristine landscape only later to be devoured by the incoming waves. As one who did not read the environmental change that was occurring, I rested on good policy and practice as the safest method for survival—I was wrong. I know now to be better prepared for the future technological aftershocks and changes due to this first storm. Yes, first storm, as there will be many more coming over the next several years.

> When I first heard, "We are thinking we need to bring in newer technologies that will support the educational process and provide a greater learning experience for our students" this was the first sign the storm would be coming.

Bring Your Own Device—Did Anyone Else Hear That Scream? Maybe It Was Just Me.

Just as iPads were hitting the scene, so too was Bring Your Own Device (BYOD)—coincidence, I think not! These iPads started another tide of change where people wanted to use their favorite devices (iPad) and do their own thing. Doesn't anyone care about security—these overblown iPhones, which are very easy to use, need to be able to connect to network services for printing, business applications, and even Windows-based applications. Good luck with that! WHAM! The next technological wave came crashing in. Virtual Desktop Infrastructure (VDI), very easy to understand concept, but very hard to build and then even worse for the user—it's more "locked down that the laptop I have." Are you kidding me? A little voice in my head spews a classic Jack Nicholson line as Colonel Jessup from the movie, *A Few Good Men,* "I have neither the time nor the inclination to explain myself to a man who rises and sleeps under the blanket of the very freedom that I provide, and then questions the manner in which I provide it! I would rather you just said thank you and went on your way." Seeing how well that played out for Colonel Jessup, I knew the same or worse outcome was in line for me unless I pulled off that blanket of security. IT had to figure out a way that would keep the network safe, and allow everyone the ability to access information from anywhere, on anything, at any time without jumping through security hoops. We introduced a virtual desktop environment that allowed these non-managed devices to access managed resources in an easy to use, bear to manage, virtual desktop solution. The product worked well, and allowed the customer to access key organizational applications on anything, from anywhere at any time—even from home.

Even though the premise of the iPads was to be the holder of any and all content needed, it wasn't long before we heard, "How do I print with these iPads?" These wonder devices that were strictly for web browsing now needed to print. We had to find a product that would allow these non-domain, unmanaged devices print on our Windows network, and it had to happen immediately. We engaged services from a third party, and implemented a product that allowed for printing from the iPads, a product which uses the Bonjour protocol, that is not well positioned for enterprise networks. As a matter of fact, network managers HATE Bonjour on their network because it is very "chatty." The term "chatty" refers to the amount of traffic generated and congestion added to the networks from non-standard protocols. I know network manager types, and they don't like to talk much, so when they refer to a protocol as "chatty" I know that's not a good thing. We have now deployed another product to allow the iPads to print, and everyone outside the network team was thrilled. We later discovered a better third party product that managed and limited the chattiness of the Bonjour protocol so much that even the network team is warming up to these new invasive devices. The schools could finally use their much-needed iPads, and now can proceed with the selection committee to rename that school in my honor.

Houston, we have a problem! Put a hold on that school naming idea—our network is crawling. Why is it so slow? That chatty protocol of Bonjour? Nope, printing is fine, and is being managed and throttled not to overtax the network, but the additional 1,500 iPads are putting a strain on the Wi-Fi. FIFTEEN HUNDRED—What? This increase accounted for a doubling effect on the number of devices on the network, but a 100-fold effect on the existing classroom Wi-Fi. The original Wi-Fi was configured and worked well for the 600 teacher laptops distributed across 12 schools. The additional concentration of 1,500 iPads in the three largest schools greatly degraded the performance of the Wi-Fi network, and this number of iPads would soon grow to over 3,000 for the remaining nine schools. Whoa!

Rising Tide of Expenses

Note to School Administration: Education grants are wonderful. They supply great resources for schools in need and when needed, BUT if it involves technology, please let your technology team know about it to prevent the next crashing wave—*BANDWIDTH.* I understand that IT can be misinterpreted as the "Department of NO," so often it is thought to ask for forgiveness rather than permission is a good method for introducing change. Not this time, this was going to be BIG! $500,000 mid-year unbudgeted kind of BIG. We needed to replace the existing Wi-Fi infrastructure that was put in place as a Wi-Fi "nice-to-have" to an enterprise level Wi-Fi dominant network. The next generation Wi-Fi had to have the capability to expand exponentially to support the increasing numbers and types of devices as well as keep pace with the additional internet bandwidth speed requirements/expectations. Since it was mid-year, we had to get creative with financing models. We chose to use a capital lease, and spread the cost over five years which was equal to the annual cost we were paying for our existing maintenance contracts on the older infrastructure. We replaced the entire network, increased Wi-Fi capabilities within six weeks, with little to no budgetary impact. Whew! Now we can finally get back to that dedication planning.

Internet of Things—Stop it!—Now You're Just Being Mean

We finally have a term that gets straight to the point. "Internet of Things" (IoT)—that's where we technologists have come to, devices and technologies are being developed, used and thrown out at alarming speeds too quickly to be named prior to obsolescence. Even the experts are tired of being late to the game with new technological naming and terminology—they've succumbed to just saying "Things." We know there are newer technologies being developed faster that we can name them so we categorize these as "Things" until we get it straight or understand where this track is taking us. So as "Things" get created and added to our environment, we must be ready, willing, and able to allow them into our networks with ease, without delays, and certainly without violating any of the numerous federally/state/educational security requirements. As buildings become "Smart", and wearable technology increases, there will be the ever-necessary need for bandwidth, but who gets priority? Most networks are now expected to carry voice, video, and data. All three forms of media carry a heavy load of bandwidth requirements and at times are a must have. So, what's required to manage all these devices requesting services appropriately? Is one more important than another? YES! But it depends on the scenario. Once again, another problem presents itself, and technology puts on its super-hero cape to the rescue. Software Defined Networks (SDN) allow for us to provision bandwidth based upon the application and priority assigned. For example, if an incident starts at the high school,

> As buildings become "Smart", and wearable technology increases, there will be the ever-necessary need for bandwidth, but who gets priority?

the public safety office needs to be able to effectively monitor activities over the video surveillance system. The bandwidth required to provide video feeds real-time will automatically be provisioned to take priority over any other bandwidth requests and present the information necessary for proper response.

All voice bandwidth provisioning is given next highest priority over data, keeping communications as the most important service running at time of an emergency. During non-emergency operations, the communication configurations of the SDN allow for the selection of bandwidth to be provided at the classroom level. All registered school-provided devices have higher bandwidth allocation over personal devices. Additional bandwidth can be provisioned from the classroom based upon a registered event. For example: if a teacher registers a classroom session for 45 minutes, the SDN will provision the classroom Wi-Fi dedicated bandwidth required for the session. All the devices registered to the specific Wi-Fi access point(s) in that classroom will be provided appropriate bandwidth requested and revert to normal operations at the end of the 45 minutes. This capability adds a tremendous amount of flexibility to the bandwidth allocation, and saves on having to overpay for bandwidth just in case it is needed. Similarly, any application that needs extra bandwidth can be set up to receive higher provisioning when used and return the bandwidth when application use has finished. Utilizing products that can measure and identify bandwidth requirements of applications and devices, we can hone in on the actual bandwidth needs of our organization. We reduced our telecommunication purchased services from three 100mb internet connections to 1 burstable 100MB connection reducing the annual operational expenses by $40,000. This available funding of $40,000 was then applied to technology equipment leases used in the classrooms.

> Software Defined Networks allow for us to provision bandwidth based upon the application and priority assigned.

Prepare for the Next Wave—It's Going to Be Even Bigger and Happen Quicker

As technologies become more advanced, and our students become more advanced, the networks, support team, and readiness will need to be greatly advanced. Often many of these requirements slip in at a constant pace and lull IT into a sense of calmness—that's the first sign the bay is emptying out, and IT will need to seek higher ground.

Seek Higher Ground: Follow the Natives Who Followed the Animals and Survived!

IT knows technology—IT needs to get with those who know the business of teaching and educating to work with them—seek higher ground—the educators are the experts, they know what they need and don't need. IT knows what technologies will help them to achieve their goals.

Most technology teams have staff that is very competent, accommodating, and occupied with existing service requests for the customers and devices supported prior to this classroom technological tsunami. Prior to the wave of classroom technology crashing into the educational landscape, seek higher ground. Higher ground will include an area of refuse for the planning of transitioning traditional-IT support to non-traditional support of IT, and be prepared—this will be the IT leader's fault. "Every man, woman, and child for themselves" will be the cry from support services when the first wave hits the classrooms. IT leaders will need to enlist customers, where technology is not their primary responsibility—"It's IT's responsibility!" For many teachers, technology will not even rank in the top ten of responsibilities or even likes. In order for the teachers/educators to be able to provide front line tier one support services for the technology that is about to crash into their professional landscape, the traditional teacher/education professional will need to learn and use this new technology. Teachers will be expected to train students on how to use this new technology, and they will need to be very involved in the day-to-day troubleshooting and support of the new technology. In a day already filled with additional job-related responsibilities, this will be the straw that breaks the camel's back if not planned properly. Teachers being accountable and responsible for the

> Teachers being accountable and responsible for the day-to-day use and support of technologies will be very important to ensure success in classroom technologies working properly.

day-to-day use and support of technologies will be very important to ensure success in classroom technologies working properly. As the IT leader, one will need to do what's necessary with the technology team to make IT better. It may involve spare inventory, professional development, and immediate remote access to assist the teachers in getting their lesson plans completed successfully. The transition of the IT support staff from specialists to generalists will be met with resistance and defiance, but stick to the plan and reassure the team, "We are all in this together, and let's make IT better."

Sunlight on Your Shores

As with all emergency preparedness planning, usually there must have been an unplanned event with great casualties for others to learn from— this is my story about how I built these recommendations for others to learn from, and hopefully not experience the pain of "learning as you go," as that into which I was cast. As service needs and expectations increase,

> IT leaders will need to work with education leadership and their staff to be able to transfer responsibilities of traditional Technical Support for these devices to the classroom.

and there is limited funding provided for these additional services, many IT leaders must provide a higher level of services without additional staff. IT leaders will need to be creative in working within the budgetary constraints to keep these initiatives viable and beneficial for education. For the 1:1 initiatives and other additional technologies in the classroom, IT leaders will need a network that can support these additional edge devices in a successful manner. IT leaders will need to work with education leadership and their staff to be able to transfer responsibilities of traditional Technical Support for these devices to the classroom. This shift in responsibilities will be met with resistance if change management is not included in the plan for this shift. IT leaders will not only need to work, coach, and educate the IT staff on the importance and needs for these changes, but they will also need to be prepared to include outside influencers such as unions, administration, elected officials, and citizens. In most cases, there are outside services (Everything as a Service) for supporting these technologies, but the point is to approach these kinds of services to augment the IT team, not to replace it. If there is a sense this is a re-placement plan, and that is not the intent, there will be no in-house support, and things can go bad very quickly. The in-house team needs to be part of the solution and included with the decision making of what is best for the organization, and how the goals of the organization and the team can coexist for everyone to be successful. There will be additional pressures to fully outsource IT, so be prepared to have facts and figures ahead of time. In most cases, there is not a financial benefit to fully-outsourced IT services.

IT leaders should look at shifts between capital expenses and operational expenses, local services to hosted services, hands on service to remote support. Professional development is not just for teachers; IT support staff will need to understand and interact with newer technologies that are specialized for educational initiatives. No longer does a single image plan work for the changing landscape of educational technologies. Resilience is brought to another level. Services are expected and required now. If services are not available, many educational initiatives will be delayed or compromised. Security vs. support needs. With everyone needing access and credentials, the need for administration's support grows exponentially. This is where security and support collide. It is against IT's nature to allow outsiders (non-IT deputized personnel) to access let alone provide the "rights" to such guarded and protected responsibilities as user access. Carefully design and plan for non-IT staffs to have appropriate rights and capabilities to support the students. This does not have to be an IT only job. Many classrooms will be experimenting with technology uses and benefits as Proof of Concepts (POCs). Many of these experiments and POC initiatives will differ from school to school, grade to grade, and possibly even classroom to classroom. Sustainable technology support starts with the educators taking on responsibility to know, understand, and resolve in-classroom technological issues. To best utilize technologies in the classroom they must be operating and used efficiently. Many traditional IT-related tasks will need to be taken on by non-traditional IT staff. Teachers, administrators, education support staff, and even students will need to be able to connect, manage, and troubleshoot the technologies in the classroom to ensure uninterrupted education time and flow of the classroom.

Focusing on the infrastructure and the core will be the direction, as well as letting go of the endpoints, but watch them carefully. IT leaders will need to handle everything at the core with policies, security. and auditing. IT leaders will need to be cautious not to get stuck in the data closet though they will need to be out with the users of technologies to ensure a smooth and successful transition. Sometimes an explanation, an email, or even a great service desk application doesn't replace the effectiveness of seeing IT in action. Get out there and engage with the customers to make IT better!

PAUL RUSSELL, *Chief Technology Officer of Town of Enfield, is responsible for the merging of technical staff, technologies, and communications of municipal, public education, and public safety entities, transitioning separately managed, locally developed, and hosted technologies to shared remote hosted vendor provided solutions. Cloud based solutions are now 80 percent of the operations. Future includes increased utilization of hosted solutions to increase resiliency and disaster recovery while reducing the risks associated with the aging infrastructure of our buildings and mechanical systems.*

Prior to municipality/education and public safety experience: Chief Technology Officer for Health Network Organizations where he managed the merging of separate health care organizations to a single medical record and enterprise-wide networks and communication systems. Application Service Providers (ASP) was the buzz word for cloud-based solutions. These solutions were the early adopter to cloud based solutions requiring Virtual Private Network (VPN) connections instead of internet connectivity.

Married 30 years to an elementary teacher—this will become important later in life as he worked with public education and got first-hand knowledge of how little his technical knowledge and expertise meant to classroom teachers. Teachers will continue to teach no matter how we try to interfere with technologies.

Father of two, one girl and one boy—one woman and one man, but they'll always be his children. Grandfather of the most adorable, beautiful little girl, Lilly Mae who is four-and-a-half, not four.

4

Implementing Technology— A Case in Point

Bobette Sylvester-McCarroll

Implementing technology is a daunting task. You have to decide what you want to do and determine if your network is designed to handle the load of the new direction and what device and software will be implemented. Then you need to know how much everything will cost, how to obtain the approval for money, and more importantly, how will teachers and students be affected and hopefully academically strengthened by the new initiative. And don't forget the most critical component—teacher training.

Now take all that complexity, and boil it down to a simple concept that can be presented to an audience of taxpayers who have little trust in government. Moreover, they want to know that the money won't be spent on the newest fad, with inherent excessive spending believed to be the root of all evil in K-12 education. In addition, you have veteran staff that is leery of new teaching methods. They have seen initiative upon initiative come and go. With all of this, you have the perfect storm, or should I say roadblock, to stop the initiative that is critical to the learning opportunities we must present to our students. This chapter is all about how to build community advocacy under today's public scrutiny of the spending of taxpayer dollars.

This is where we started. In our district, we were faced with implementing a new direction of technology in the classroom which previously had been minimal in nature. We were in a very conservative, traditional community and school culture, although we were the largest district in the state. The district was seen as a model for its implementation of standards-based curriculum and teacher training but had not implemented much in the way of blended learning or student use of technology in the classroom.

Know What the Problem You're Trying to Solve Is

Luckily for our students, the Governing Board and Superintendent recognized the emerging need for our students to be technology literate. In addition, individualized instruction was coming to the forefront of importance to student achievement. Added to this was the critical need of individualization and the diversity of our population in both ethnicity and poverty. Many of our students did not have the same access to technology as their peers in the classroom, and our minority population was not increasing in academic gains at the same rate of their peers in other districts.

Now comes the buy-in problem. We had the Governing Board strongly supporting the need for technology in the classroom, and we had a conceptual idea of what we wanted to accomplish. What we didn't have was the details of the plan or the costs. Of course, this is where we all begin.

Develop a Strong Cohesive Team that Owns the Problem

We started out with a small team of cohesive leaders, our Assistant Superintendent for Curriculum and Instruction, our Technology Director, the Information Systems Director, the Purchasing Director and me, the Assistant Superintendent of Business Support Services. What seemed unique in our situation was that three of the five were new to our positions with two veterans; however, all on the team had an openness to change balanced with the knowledge of what was done in the past and the current culture.

Critically important was the strong collaboration between the business and curriculum sides of the house. Often, Information Systems with the need to protect and maintain stability to the network become conflicted with the Educational Technology Department that need a responsive, flexible system that can adapt to change and integrate multiple different academic resources. However, these two professionals worked closely together with a shared strong work ethic, belief in the

> Often, Information Systems with the need to protect and maintain stability to the network become conflicted with the Educational Technology Department that need a responsive, flexible system that can adapt to change and integrate multiple different academic resources.

teaching profession, and mutual respect that was critical to the team. In addition, an initiative cannot be successful if you don't include the department that facilitates the purchases, and our Purchasing Director became a driver to the details of contracts and delivery timelines as well as our leader in assisting with the deployment of devices. Finally, the Assistant Superintendent of Curriculum and Instruction already saw the need for more digital resources and drove the vision behind the need for teacher development. Matching her passion for teaching was my passion for technology. We were able to leverage my skills of budget preparation, board and community communication, and contract negotiations. Together, we were an incredibly strong team of five.

Build the Details of the Plan and Do the Work

So, I go back to the challenge, getting a buy-in from all your constituents: board, staff, students, and community. We started with a visioning process that had previously been led with a small group of our constituents with the support of Cisco. This was an overarching look at the needs and future aspirations of the use of technology in the classroom. We used this as a framework as the five of us started meeting every two weeks for two hour blocks.

Some of our direction was simply organic as we would bounce issues against possible solutions, and part was of each member doing the research looking for best practices. With every member personally committed to the success of each initiative and understanding the important of their specific role, we had the power of not five but many.

We quickly determined that we had three critical needs. One, we had to completely redesign our network to ensure both security and flexibility, as well as pervasive wireless capabilities to every site; 87 in total. Second, we had to help start a culture of technology use in the classroom at a grassroots level that could be scaled. And finally, we needed the resources to support the first two.

In our state of Arizona, we bounce around the lowest three states in the country on per pupil funding. To make matters worse, after the great recession, our capital funding was cut by 86 percent. The only opportunity to move ahead with this type of initiative was to ask our constituents to pass a bond. This is an election where the local constituents agree to have their property taxes raised to support the funding for any building or technology needs. Given that we needed extensive cabling for wireless access points, reconfiguration of network closets, as well as hardware for both the network and devices for teachers and students, we had the needs for both. The team used the professional knowledge of our Information Systems staff as well as an outside consultant to redesign the network and come up with estimated costs. In addition, we estimated the need for a 1:2 student-to-device ratio over the upcoming five years. Putting cabling, hardware, and devices together, it was a whopping bill of $67,000,000 Although that supported 64,000 students, it seemed huge if it wasn't put into context. In addition, this was the deeply discounted price we hoped to achieve through partnership. Not a small undertaking to communicate and achieve buy-in from a very conservative community.

Clearly and Consistently Tell Your Story

Knowing that we needed the buy-in from all areas within our organization, we started consistently communicating with staff the direction from the Governing Board and Superintendent as well as our understanding of the need to support teachers and students along the journey. Articulating that we basically had a superhighway of bandwidth (speed availability) that became a dirt road as soon as it reached the building was an easy sell; teachers were very frustrated by their lack of access to most anything Internet. We needed a new network and extensive wireless. Emphasizing that technology was simply a tool, one of many to help with student engagement and leaning wasn't so hard either. We were honest that at that time, little research could show a direct correlation of implementing technology with student achievement. However, we did speak of the gains technology brought with student engagement, fewer absences, and less student discipline. The ability to differentiate instruction and utilize a learning management system that was becoming common place in the university and college settings down into the high school level was critical.

However, a little harder was the safety and security of student information and access. And the hardest was the knowledge that any of these initiatives would fail if we did not bring teachers along in the design, selection, and training process.

Use Committee Input and Process for Potential Advocates

So, we knew that if we made it relevant to our students, we engaged our teachers and staff, and if we communicated in a simple, honest, and consistent way we could start the ball rolling. We did so by embedding the story of our need and direction into our Facilities Planning Committee process. This was a 52-member committee of principals, city leaders, teachers, staff, students, parents, and community members that were part of our process to recommend to the Governing Board the total amount needed for the upcoming bond. We used a committee process to both educate our constituents to the extensive needs of the district as well as used their feedback and review of schools to develop a comprehensive master facilities plan. This committee did not have the latitude into any recommendation for the technology plan, but they were a venue for us to tell the story of our needs and vision as part of their total bond recommendation. After three months, many two-hour meetings, and extensive presentation of information and nonpartisan facilitated discussion, the committee recommended the largest bond in our state's history. The Governing Board passed a resolution in the fall of 2012 to put a bond of $230,000,000 bond on the ballot for a voter decision.

By empowering this committee to make a recommendation to the Governing Board as to the amount of the upcoming bond, we had natural advocates into the community to tell the story of our facility needs as well as our technology needs. A Political Action Committee was established by supporters of our schools to help promote the bond and communicate the use of funds. Meetings were held at every school site to educate attendees and address concerns and used a simple PowerPoint presentation to keep the message consistent and simple. Direct mailers and extensive signage helped round out the campaign, and voters passed the bond with a 64 percent rate. This was a huge success in a district where 67 percent of our voters were 50 years of age or older.

Now that we had funding, the hard work of design and implementation had to take place.

Engage Your Site Leaders

Our first venture was to update all of our administrator's technology with iPads. This was a step that allowed us to test that device as well as to spark the use of technology with our site leaders. We've seen specific results that if the site leader believes in the power of technology, the use and expansion are exponential compared to leaders that are uncomfortable with it.

Empower Your Forward-Thinking Teachers

Next, working with our superintendent's vision of opening up our process and empowering our teachers to test technology, we sponsored a technology fair in the spring of 2013. This was a powerful test of combining a procurement process for hardware and software wrapped around a two-day technology "convention" where we brought in teachers to preview the items. To enhance participation, we incorporated an application process where after attending our technology fair teams of teachers could submit plans for funding to implement technology in their classroom. That fall we funded twelve innovation teams. These teams were varied in their approach from grade levels to areas of instruction. In addition, they all wanted to use various resources and devices. I believe this process was our first specific success. It empowered our teachers who were more technology literate to pilot in their classrooms as a grassroots effort, and more importantly, allowed us to both succeed and fail on a much smaller level. We learned many lessons on how to integrate hardware, coordinate student database information, manage software vendors who many times promised what couldn't be quickly achieved, and how to support our teachers who were brave enough to step into new teaching methods. It was as exciting as it was scary.

In addition to the innovation teams, we also took our lowest performing elementary school, and remade it into an Innovation School. A new administrator was hired with a technology focus, and all teachers were either allowed to transfer or re-interviewed for a position on this campus. The site was renovated for flexible classrooms, and E-Rate funds were used for infrastructure upgrades. We used this school to pilot all Apple platforms.

At the same time this was happening, we were managing multiple cabling vendors to install switches and wireless access points across all schools and departments. Given our poverty rates, we specifically designed coverage in all areas including open areas such as our parking lots and football fields. We wanted to ensure that even if school wasn't in session that as we moved into a Bring Your Own Device (BYOD) or 1:1 environment, our students could find wireless access afterhours. Utilizing E-Rate enabled us to increase our bandwidth to a potential five devices per student.

Keep Your Initiative Moving—Hold Your Promises

This was all in the first 14 months after the bond passed. Although that much change and construction was daunting, we had to move quickly to ensure that the promises we made through the bond process were adhered to, and that teachers saw the impact as soon as the resources were determined to be viable. Toward that end, the next step was to start thinking about how to move to a larger scale of implementation and towards a 1:1 environment that would allow students to take devices home. We had many discussion of BYOD versus 1:1 with district supplied devices. In the end given the diversity of communities and the difficulty to support different devices from a teacher and technician's perspective, we decided to standardize on one device.

Involve and Ask for Teachers' Input

We also decided that we needed to support our teachers with deploying devices to them first, and with extensive teacher training prior to deploying to students beyond those who were part of the original innovation teams. This was intentional to ensure teachers were comfortable with their devices prior to adding the stress of students having devices in the classroom. We also decided that to be successful, given how quickly we were moving, we needed to create a process for teacher input into the device selection. Utilizing our strong procurement department, we used a process to narrow down our options to three devices. We then created mock classrooms for teachers to come touch, test, and utilize the devices. They rotated through three different classrooms, and then we surveyed them for their opinions. In addition, we tested the devices in our high school's vocational classrooms for two days, looking at battery life, ease of use, keyboard functionality, etc., and we also surveyed the students. After a successful negotiation and partnership discussion, we were ready to order and deploy 4,000 devices to teachers in our second year.

Know Your Numbers and Margins

I've mentioned twice the concept of partnership and negotiation. This is critical to an initiative of this size. Clearly articulating the scale of this type of venture, the purchasing value and the opportunities for promotion if the pricing and timelines are adhered to benefits both parties. In addition, given that contracts are public record and board approved, taking the time to work with vendors and partners to negotiate prices and services is part of gaining the respect of your community as they can evaluate the value brought to the district. Know your percentage discount from market prices, and better yet, know your discounts compared to peer districts. Communicating an average discount from market rate of 64 percent or $45,000,000 is powerful information to your constituents.

> Taking the time to work with vendors and partners to negotiate prices and services is part of gaining the respect of your community as they can evaluate the value brought to the district.

Communicate and Update

Another critical element is to consistently monitor the initiatives and update the Governing Board. We've discussed the progress at almost every meeting. In addition, we developed a five-year plan that we reviewed and updated annually. We also had various presentations to the Governing Board and to the public from our innovation teams, educational technology trainers, Innovation School, etc.

Be Flexible

Right before we were getting ready to deploy to teachers and with the lessons from our innovation teams, we stumbled on our next big "aha." If we were going to really change how teaching looked, we had to move teachers away from their desks, devices, and projectors. Our answer was Wi-Fi. Utilizing a wireless projector with a tablet device "untethered" teachers, and allowed them to move about the classroom while teaching. Although we stumbled across this huge paradigm shift shortly before the deployment of devices to teachers, it was important to implement them both at the same time. Had we waited a year to implement this part of our initiative, I believe we would have lost tremendous value in helping out teachers understand the power of flexibility that being untethered could bring to their teaching styles and student engagement.

All of this planning and implementing was nice, but was only the first step to our originally identified want—to have technologically competent students. That was the major goal, and after two and a half years of work, we were ready for the next big step—students with devices.

Buy Thoughtfully

We had many discussions as a small group initially on the type of devices that should be purchased. Many different products were emerging, and pricing seemed to be driving the market. However, we had concerns about device storage, workforce software basics, cloud storage if a student didn't have wireless at home, management or barriers to apps, etc. Therefore, we finally settled on Lenovo tablet that carried Microsoft products that met all the above needs. Although it was costlier than iPad or Chromebook devices, we felt the investment for our students was better with a full computer tablet.

So, moving into our third year it was time to deploy devices into the classroom. We started out by purchasing three carts of devices for every elementary school and carts with devices for every English classroom at the 7-12 grades. In addition, we had high schools apply to be a true 1:1 school where students were assigned a device and would take them home each night. Our schools' plans had to include elements of teacher training, utilization goals, and estimated outcomes. After reviewing the submissions, we made a selection, and in the fall of 2015 we launched our first 1:1 school.

Please don't be misled into thinking this was an easy task. In this year, we purchased 18,600 devices. We deployed 3,100 devices to high school students five days prior to the school start. We utilized every staff member on our team to cover the deployment strategies, help in the bookstore processing optional device protection fees, download textbook materials, and activate student Active Directory accounts. It was a mammoth effort in scope, but the school's leadership, staff, and our teams were committed to its success.

It was so successful, that our second high school that had been selected as a Fall 2016 implementation asked to be moved up to second semester of 2015, deploying 2,500 devices in January. We also learned lessons from a mid-year implementation, but again, with committed leadership and staff it was successful.

Over this season, we refined some of our processes, and enhanced our summer learning institute for 2016 by modeling what we were asking teachers to do and offered our sessions in a blended format utilizing our District's learning management system. This was modeling for our staff in the best way possible. Yes, you should eat what you serve.

Protect Your Assets and the Communities' Trust

Arizona's Constitution provides for a free public education. Therefore, we were prohibited from charging for the use of a device. However, we could charge for the loss or damage of a device. So, based on research on other districts' successful implementations, we created our own Device Protection Plan. This allowed us to offer a plan that would cover the costs if a student's device were damaged or stolen. This was an optional plan for students, but each student who received a device signed a document stating the policies covering technology use as well as the costs if the device was damaged. It then allowed students to purchase a protection plan or waive its fee.

This must have been fairly appealing to students and parents who were accustomed to similar problems or costs with cell phones as 87 percent of our students purchased this plan in the first full year that we implemented 1:1.

Tracking our statistics and promoting it to our public, we had a 2.3 percent total loss of devices that year, and only an 11 percent damage rate. The money collected from the Device Protection Plan covered all the costs of repairs.

Keep Adapting and Moving

In the fourth year, we implemented two more 1:1 high schools, deploying a total of 12,000 devices to our four high schools. Two schools deployed the week prior to the start of school, and two schools deployed during the first week of school. At the junior high school level, we added enough carts for every student in every math classroom to have a device. As a side note, they almost have enough devices at an 83 percent saturation rate that they could go 1:1. but we're not ready for our junior high school students to take them home at this time. In addition, we deployed additional carts and devices to our elementary schools based on population so that every elementary had a saturation rate of 43 percent. In total, we are now managing 35,000 devices as well as other technologies within the Internet of Things.

Our goal next year is to deploy 1:1 at our two remaining high schools.

Celebrate Your Successes and Own Your Failures

This short timeline of five years says nothing of the amount of work and the number of people many people were involved to make this a success. And we've had some failures. With the exponential growth, we had adequate bandwidth, but not enough storage. We are currently growing two terabytes every week. What a wonderful/awful problem to have.

Anticipating that issue, we migrated data into new services, but have had a difficult Fall undoing some of the policies we set in the beginning to help ensure teachers didn't lose saved data. In the end, we've lost some in the new transition. We own that.

However, those bruises have led us to understand the importance of moving our student information into the cloud and reinforced the need to train our teachers on file storage and backups. We've also benefited from a stronger trust relationship that we built with staff in the beginning by being extremely responsive and flexible to their needs. This has served us well as we went through a bumpy Fall start.

Although we have limited staff, we've maximized our service support with the use of a consultant for best design and partnered with the educational technology staff for site support. We added additional contract teachers for online instructional delivery coaches, hired 50 students over the summer for reimaging and maintenance of devices, and finally in this fifth year added additional 21 staff members to support the hardware and curriculum sides of the house. This nearly doubled the staff we had for the first four years. More hands do make a difference.

Conclusion

So, as you can tell, there isn't one perfect or easy strategy to get commitments, either with money or buy in, within your community. And your community extends to many areas, staff, teachers, students, parents, tax payers, and politicians. However, with an empowered team, careful strategies, passion, and hard work, you can set forth on the path of the true win, helping students become technologically literate, differentiating instruction in the classroom, and closing the achievement gap with diverse populations. In the end, that's all that matters.

BOBETTE SYLVESTER-MCCARROLL *joined Mesa Public Schools in July, 2011 as the Assistant Superintendent for Business and Support Services. In this capacity, she directs a host of financial and business activities ranging from budget development, facilities construction and maintenance, payroll, accounts receivable and payable to technology services, student transportation, food services, purchasing, and the material distribution center. She was previously noted in the Arizona Republic Newspaper's Top Newsmakers in Mesa in 2012 for her direction of a diverse 37-member facilities planning committee as part of the bond planning and approval process.*

Bobette currently serves as the President of the Arizona Schools Risk Retention Trust. Previously she has served on the Board of the Arizona Association of School Business Officials as the Past President, and was formerly on the Board for the Payson Regional Medical Center. In addition, she has served as a member of the School Finance Advisory Committee for the Arizona Auditor General's Office, and on an advisory committee for the Governor's Office on school finance. Prior to working 16 years as the Assistant Superintendent for Business Services for Payson Unified School District, she worked in the valley as a financial analyst for a private sector firm. She received her Bachelor of Science degree in Accounting for Arizona State University, and is a Certified Public Accountant.

5

Overcoming Roadblocks and Embracing Innovation
A Framework for Action:
The Future and How to Get There

Renee Patton

It should now be clear that K-12 as an industry is in the midst of a monumental change. The potential for disruption in this market segment is high as new technologies, as well as a new generation of students come onto the scene. Do students really need to attend classes in person? Why aren't video-recorded lectures and other course materials readily available to help students learn more effectively and reach students who may not be able to attend class, or who might need to review concepts more than once? And is there a way we can better personalize the learning experience for students?

Often and ironically, when major disruptions occur, the incumbent is surprised: think Uber and the taxi industry, Air B&B and hotels, and Zillow and traditional real estate firms. Many educators understand the current change dynamics, and are moving swiftly to innovate and transform the instructional delivery model, in light of the changing role of teachers, the students of the future, and the need to prepare students for college and career readiness. Others may still be of the mind that modest incremental shifts are all that are necessary, which could result in them not being here to witness the next generation of education.

To survive and realize success in the future, forward-thinking K-12 leaders across the nation need to find new and innovative ways to engage students and faculty, meet students where they are with personalized learning approaches, and effectively prepare students for college and career, while simultaneously finding funding for new teaching and learning initiatives.

Change is difficult, but we have found it helpful to provide concrete recommendations on how district leaders can further the dialogue to transform their institutions for the future, and safeguard against surprise, with a framework for action.

Common Challenges and the Role of Technology

Educators and administrators share a common crisis in the delivery of learning. They suffer many of the same challenges, with regard to access to quality educational experiences, the need to evolve outdated teaching methodologies, the imperative to prepare students for college or to become part of the workforce of the future, increasing costs, decreasing funds, and a generation of students who are continuing to tune-out and turn-off from the traditional approach of age-old instructional methods.

Technology and the massive shift to digital play key roles in enabling new ways of learning and new business models required to drive the very transformation that schools are trying to effect. Technology can support new learning approaches that engage learners, drive new revenue streams, decrease operational costs, and preserve and expand the a school or district's brand.

In many K-12 districts, technology is still relegated to a standalone silo, where Chief Information Officers (CIOs), directors of technology, and their staff are frustrated by the pace of change, the lack of resource and funding, and the challenge of translating the benefits that technology brings to the business of the institution and to teaching and learning. But today, technology can no longer be left alone in a silo because it is literally the lifeblood of the successful district.

Importantly, the CIO and technology teams can't do it alone. They need the support of the Superintendent, Assistant Superintendents, Principals, faculty members and the community

> Technology can support new learning approaches that engage learners, drive new revenue streams, decrease operational costs, and preserve and expand the a school or district's brand.

to lead and effect change. While the Superintendent doesn't necessarily need to be actively engaged in the day-to-day activities around change initiatives, he or she certainly needs to take a strong leadership position, helping to set the vision, advocating for change, and providing full support to the CIO and other designated leaders of the change.

Technology also plays an important role in supporting and driving actual change initiatives. Very simply, technology enables better connections, easier communication paths, and more robust collaboration. It helps create environments that make it easier for change makers to share ideas, discuss possible approaches, and meet consistently and frequently without the barriers of time, distance, or cost.

Design Principles

While there is a multitude of paths that K-12 districts can take to transform, these design principles are critical for all K-12 leaders to consider.

A Vision for the Future

Having an understanding of the future state makes it easier to plan. We spend a great deal of our time working with K-12 leaders, sharing trends and technologies that are shaping the future of education, and helping them imagine the possible.

It helps leaders identify key "impact areas" that they would like to affect, to prioritize focus and investment, and to determine the type of experience they would like to deliver across all constituents: faculty, administrative leaders, students, staff, and the community. Imagining the day in the life of each of these stakeholder audiences makes the intended changes real, and is an important step in the planning process.

It is important to have the right people involved in the visioning process; many of these individuals will naturally become standing members of the Task Force that implements the strategy and plan:

- The School Board who is responsible for managing district policy and budget, and who will ultimately sign off on major capital expenditures often required for optimal transformation. These members are also an important link to the community, their base of constituents responsible for putting them in the political offices they hold;

- The Superintendent who normally already has a clear vision of the future (although this vision may not include a fully technology-enabled environment);
- Faculty members who are using technology today, and faculty members who would like to use technology, but haven't made the jump. It might also be good to include naysayers who, although skeptical, have a history of embracing change once convinced of its value.
- CFOs and Chief Business Officers who will help identify the resources for the change, assist with business use cases, and return on investment (ROI) and total cost of ownership (TCO) models, taking into account specific state and federal regulations;
- Chief Academic Officers who are responsible for providing the best learning experiences possible and driving student success and learning outcomes;
- Facilities Managers and Safety and Security Officers who can help identify opportunities for the Internet of Things technologies, such as connected heating, lighting and transportation;
- CIOs and information technology personnel who can provide insights into the current state of technology, what is possible with technology, and what will be required to execute against the district vision;
- Key technology partners who can share future trends, current technologies, and ways to leverage technology investments across the operation while creating comprehensive connected teaching, learning, and campus environments.
- Current students who are a part of the learning community;
- Alums and other interested community members who have an interest in helping the district thrive into the future.

Identify the Champion for Change
The Superintendent and his or her senior leaders will set the tone for change and demand action, but the champion for change will probably be someone else.

While the CIO will likely be the functional leader of the change, the champion for change might be someone else. Consider an Assistant

Superintendent, a Principal, or leaders of other successful initiatives on campus. Think about who has led successfully in the past, who has rallied the troops, who is liked and respected by his or her peers. The champion should be someone who understands the complexity of the organization while simultaneously helping people internalize the sense of urgency.

The champion could be a highly-motivated faculty member who is using technology today, and would like to see broader implementation across the campus. He or she could also conceivably be a former student, a customer of the institution, who comes on board to help create passion, urgency, and understanding of the need for change.

The successful champion will work to firmly establish the vision, created and set by the broader team, and then to put this vision into motion. He or she will help propagate understanding across multiple departments for the need to change, breaking down silos and identifying other like-minded individuals. The champion will stick with driving the initiative until it's complete.

> Because the creation of new technologies is rapidly accelerating, it makes sense to have innovation groups established to vet new trends and technologies and find ways to appropriately incorporate them into the overall vision and plan.

Committees, Task Forces, and Innovation Groups

After the vision is set, the work to deliver on the vision begins. Different districts will develop different ways to create the plan, plan the work and work the plan. Having a strategic task force, supported by a limited number of committees organized by defined goals, to drive the overall vision and plan works well. A cadence of communication with weekly or bi-weekly meetings or checkpoints is important to hold committee leaders responsible for key milestones and deliverables, and it's critical that the champion be provided with a program or project manager to help execute against the plan.

Because the creation of new technologies is rapidly accelerating, it makes sense to have innovation groups established to vet new trends and technologies and find ways to appropriately incorporate them into the overall vision and plan.

Student Experience Drives Exponential Change

Student success is one of the most important goals in K-12 today, and students themselves, when bought into a vision, can help to drive change exponentially. Several factors affect how and when change will occur, but the approach that K-12 districts take to implement and integrate technology into the core fabric of the institution is an increasingly important factor in driving student learning outcomes.

Today's students demand always-on access to the network and resources and information needed to realize success. They expect extreme speed and reliability in their wireless connections, and a simple and seamless online interface to their courses, academic and administrative information and student services. They want access to information when they need it and where they can most easily find it. And they want to attend classes anytime, anywhere. They don't necessarily want to physically attend every class.

> Students are your customers; as such, it is critical to ensure their views are represented.

The extent to which a K-12 district can deliver this type of experience will enable change to occur faster. Today's students don't want to attend schools with technology that is absent or lacking, technology that is unable to deliver a robust student experience. To this point, it is strongly recommended that you include one or more students in different grade levels as a part of the stakeholder community. Students are your customers; as such, it is critical to ensure their views are represented.

Communicate, Collaborate, or Fail

The fact that many K-12 districts continue to operate in siloes is a major factor that inhibits change. Communication and collaboration foster diversity of thought, encourages action and improves understanding—all core values of a quality education.

District leaders must be able to communicate and collaborate more effectively with one another to share ideas and best practices, and discuss ways to address their most pressing challenges.

Most importantly, a high level of collaboration must exist between leaders and their faculty and staff. Including the faculty perspective and their ownership of change is critical. We know in our work with K-12 districts of all types and sizes across the country and globe that if this doesn't happen, change will be less than successful.

Finally, students must be able to easily communicate and collaborate with one another, their teachers and outside experts. For a generation that thrives on community and connection to one another, districts must make it easy for students to connect with their communities, whether other students in a class, mentors, colleges or anyone else who makes up their social network.

> Technology can help break down the walls that have traditionally existed in education, and can help make collaboration easier and more ubiquitous.

Technology can help break down the walls that have traditionally existed in education, and can help make collaboration easier and more ubiquitous. The ability to hold online meetings, deliver collaborative work spaces, and utilize video across the campus helps people to connect better, and enables more frequent sharing of best practices, course design approaches, and access to outside expertise. Not having to travel across campus makes it easier for leaders to meet, faculty members to hold office hours and other meetings, and students to work with one another or their teachers.

Technology Improves Efficiency

For cash-strapped K-12 districts, technology can help save time and money, freeing up funds for investment in newer technologies that can transform the district. Technology can enable better administrative efficiency, helping faculty, staff, and administrators to meet anytime, anywhere, and on any device. Rather than investing in travel for teachers spread across a large district, for example, meetings can take place over the web with high-quality video conferencing tools.

These same video and collaboration tools can be multi-purposed to offer students virtual courses, to deliver concurrent enrollment programs with community colleges, to bring outside experts into the district, and to scale scarce teaching resources across a district. Why hire five AP calculus teachers across five different schools that have varying level of demand for calculus on each campus when one high-quality teacher can offer courses to all five schools over immersive telepresence video?

Finally, new sensor technology can be used to monitor and control heating, ventilation, and air conditioning systems, automatically turning these on only as needed. Connected school transportation solutions can optimize pick-up routes for school busses and determine the efficiency of busses, all while keeping students safe and secure.

The Internet of Things really will change everything

The Internet of Things (IoT) is the networked connection of people, process, data and things, and represents the confluence of multiple technology trends: mobility (ubiquitous, high-speed mobile networks, smart devices, and apps), cloud computing, social networks, instant collaboration with anyone, anywhere; data analytics, and finally, an explosion in connected "things" via inexpensive, intelligent sensors. IoT brings these elements together with standards-based IP networks, and Cisco projects that it will generate a staggering $19,000,000,000,000 in value over the next ten years. Of this, $258,000,000,000 of the IoT value-at-stake will come from solutions for Connected Learning alone.[1]

The network, which is at the heart of IoT, must be stable, scalable, reliable and capable of handling the increased rate of traffic from the explosion of mobile devices, the use of video and the implementation of new applications for communications and collaboration. It must be safe, secure, wired and wireless, easy to manage and administer, and it must be designed to meet future growth requirements. The Internet of Things helps customers to accelerate the creation of connected learning experiences.

A Framework for Action

We realize that there are a multitude of different planning processes and frameworks available today. We have used the following framework to help our K-12 customers move very quickly and successfully through the major market transitions they are experiencing and to turn vision into reality.

From helping to define a vision and identifying gaps to providing a unifying technology architectural design and comprehensive set of solutions that address these gaps, Cisco and our partners help our schools

---

[1] http://www.cisco.com/c/dam/en_us/services/portfolio/consulting-services/documents/consulting-services-capturing-ioe-value-aag.pdf

create a completely integrated digital environment. Cisco's solutions and services for digital learning and the digital campus are enabled by the Cisco Digital Education Platform (DEP) comprised of a secure core network, unified voice, state-of-the-art wireless and security everywhere. The Cisco DEP is the foundation for change.

Whether flipping, capturing, or enhancing courses, faculty members can quickly and simply create and schedule classes, and use our leading-edge video and collaboration tools to fully engage students. Educators can leverage the same technology to optimize and streamline access, develop smart workspaces and intelligent facilities, and create safer, more secure campuses.

We have found, in fact, that this framework increases the likelihood of success for major change initiatives.

Framework Overview

At a high level, district technology change initiatives typically include the following phases:

Phase 1: Set the vision –develop a "future-state view"
- Establish a foundation for change;
- Identify goals and gaps;
- Design and establish the infrastructure;
- Develop service-ready architectures.

Phase 2: Analyze the financial impact
- Define key impact areas that increase revenue and decrease cost;
- Conduct financial modeling and ROI simulations;
- Confirm the business case.

Phase 3: Implement solutions to expand services, adoption and utilization
- Implement solutions to drive adoption and gain expertise;
- Leverage new applications and services to lay the groundwork for transformation.

Phase 4: Support the transformation—integrated solutions support transformation
- Leverage new, integrated solutions to support transformation on business and learning;
- Improve learning outcomes;
- Create excellent learning environments for students.

Detailed Framework—STEPS

This step-by-step framework will assist with the definition and execution of major change initiatives.

1. Develop a stakeholder community using the following as considerations (many or most of these individuals will come from the visioning team):
   a. Include individuals from the district who will be helping to lead the change initiative or who will be impacted by the change;
   b. Make sure that executive administrators are included, including the Superintendent, Assistant Superintendents, Chief Business Officer (CBO), Chief Financial Officer (CFO), Chief Information Officer (CIO), Principals, and other key decision makers;
   c. Include department chairs and key faculty members with a mix of perspectives;
   d. Consider including students so that they can represent the student experience;
   e. Think about connections to the local community and include representatives from community colleges, other K-12 districts, community foundations and organizations, and regional education networks as appropriate;
   f. Include key, trusted technology partners who have enabled change in other organizations such as yours, and who can share best practices and help you in your journey. Expand the definition of partners, including technology vendors, non-profits and other organizations that have an interest in the district's vision and strategy.
2. Implement tools that will drive collaboration, engage the community and help enable more effective implementation of change

a. Consider obtaining Cisco WebEx or the equivalent to help your stakeholder community to connect and collaborate on a regular basis, without having to travel;

b. Utilize technologies such as Cisco Telepresence or the equivalent for high-definition, high-quality meetings;

c. Leverage free Cisco Spark licenses to engage with your broader community, track action items, and create team spaces via high-quality, low-cost collaboration and video tools.

3. With the design considerations above, work with the stakeholder community to clearly define the district vision. Ask yourselves these questions:

a. What does the future hold, and how will it impact me and my institution?

b. What are the major trends and transitions that we have to consider to survive and thrive?

c. How will I differentiate my district from others?

d. How can I deliver the best student experience in the industry?

e. What types of experiences do we want to deliver to faculty, staff, and students, such as the ability:

    i. For students to take classes anywhere, anytime, on any device;

    ii. To deliver a range of learning models, including online, hybrid, and flipped learning;

    iii. To connect with outside experts and bring them into courses as lecturers or guest teachers;

    iv. To work with other schools and districts in my area, the state, or the nation to share courses, content, and teachers, thus increasing the number of courses we can offer and the number of students we can serve;

    v. For faculty, staff, and students to connect seamlessly to the network;

    vi. To ensure a safe, secure, and reliable network;

    vii. To ensure student safety across the campus.

    viii. For faculty, staff, and students to connect and collaborate regardless of location.

f. How can our partners help?

g. What are potential funding sources for the work that we do?

h. Where can we save money and increase funding streams?

i. What will success look like once you've implemented your plan and executed against your vision? In other words, what are your success metrics?

4. Identify and replicate best practices that are working in other districts

   a. Your partners are some of the best sources of these best practices, and most have broad libraries of case studies that you can reference. In the case of Cisco, for example, you can see how:

      i. Paradise Valley implemented a major video initiative to serve students across the district by offering a range of courses over video and by connecting with the national education research network and select universities;

      ii. ITASCA area school district used video and collaboration technologies to offer courses to students in remote and rural locations, and used the same technologies for better and more frequent staff meetings;

      iii. Katy Independent School District rolled out one of the fastest, most reliable, and most effective wireless networks in the country.

5. Outline major strategic initiatives that will drive transformation across the district

   a. Clearly define your major areas of strategic impact;

   b. Identify requirements across the community to achieve your vision and strategy;

   c. Define required tactics for each strategy and determine how you will measure success.

6. Obtain broad buy-in and agreement on the vision and strategy

   a. Use collaboration tools to communicate the vision and strategy;

   b. Work with partners who can help you to visually represent you vision and obtain greater buy-in.

7. Within the plan, define technologies and solutions that will enable you to:

   a. Address the requirements outlined in the vision and strategy;

   b. Transform the district;

    c. Help accelerate and scale the transformation;

    d. Take an architectural approach to reduce cost, minimize risk, and remove complexity.

8. Consider the following technologies that can help realize your plan:

    a. Broadband access and network connectivity allows districts with schools in remote areas to expand access to education and resources for faculty members and students;

    b. Increased bandwidth and security enables districts to consolidate administration services to improve reliability and reduce operational costs;

    c. A solid core infrastructure serves as the foundation for all IoT applications;

    d. Improved system integration and interoperability improve ease of upgrades and expansion;

    e. Wireless networks provide reliable and secure ubiquitous Internet access regardless of location on campus;

    f. Lecture capture allows recording of and future review of classroom content;

    g. Video capabilities enable faculty and students to connect across disparate locations and allow for the inclusion of guest lecturers and virtual field trips in courses;

    h. Video and collaboration technologies improve communications between faculty and staff and allow for deeper and more frequent professional development opportunities;

    i. Collaboration technologies increase avenues of collaborative learning, with significant cost savings.

Stakeholder Checklists

It is helpful to consider what each stakeholder in the district might need from his or her unique perspective.

Superintendent/Assistant Superintendents

- Connect and communicate with the broader community;
- Show the value of the vision, strategy, and related investment, including return on investment, total cost of ownership and other financial metrics that can be reviewed with the Board;
- Robust technologies that help engage both teachers and students.

CIO/Facilities/Safety and Security
- Robust, reliable and scalable wired and wireless network;
- Safe and secure data network and physical campus;
- Physical room systems and campus facilities that take advantage of new IoT technologies to increase efficiency and decrease cost;
- Faculty and staff training on how to use new technologies;
- Incentives to help effect change and encourage others to become change advocates.

Principals
- Ability to articulate the vision;
- A way to engage teachers in change processes;
- Improving learning outcomes at their specific schools.

Department Chairs
- Faculty awareness training;
- Faculty champions and incentives to help drive change;
- Online subscriptions to media;
- Software packages for associated hardware technologies.

CBO/CFO
- Understanding use cases as it applies to the mission of the district;
- Financial implications and leveragability of investments;
- Adherence to state and federal rules/regulations;
- TCO and ROI models.

Conclusion

Transforming education has been discussed for decades, and many revolutionary ideas have been met with skepticism. The lexicon of education administration today simmers with the vocabulary of change. Change is difficult, and collectively understanding exactly what we are trying to change, why we are trying to change it, and what the ideal state would look like when we are finished are big tasks.

Breaking down organizational silos is a fundamental aspect of this change, and sometimes seems impossible; but defining a vision for the future, and helping people understand the need for change, can be highly rewarding as previous skeptics embrace change initiatives and become a part of the solution that seemed impossible becomes more probable.

While change is difficult, it's not impossible, and as discussed throughout this book, we, as a society, have no choice but to change. In the spirit of imagining the possible, think about the type of business models that will be most effective to enable and support the experiences we want for everyone involved in the journey of learning.

Administrative leaders who guide districts that operate efficiently and effectively with a greater degree of agility to adjust to the changing world around us; teaching and learning environments that are taking advantage of a variety of technology solutions to better engage our students, and prepare our next generation workforce; and an environment of innovation that allows both teachers and students to create novel new learning environments for today and for tomorrow.

As Winston Churchill said, "Success is not final, failure is not fatal: it is the courage to continue that counts."

RENEE PATTON *is the leader of US Public Sector Education at Cisco. She and her team help schools, colleges and universities envision the future of learning and start planning and executing on their vision today. With over 20 years of business, management, sales and marketing experiences in both small start-ups and large corporations, Renee has managed through adversity and diversity to help customers realize technology solutions that drive business outcomes.*

Including a Master's Degree in Education from Stanford, Renee has spent 18 years in education, giving her a clear perspective to address business issues and changing landscapes. Always a curious learner herself, it was after earning her undergraduate degree that she became a high school English and French teacher. She coached cross-country, and moderated the student yearbook and newspaper, becoming deeply ingrained in the school culture. She then spent four years on the district side managing policy and a $20,000,000 budget for Los Gatos-Saratoga JUHS Board of Trustees, learning firsthand how a district runs and understanding regional challenges.

6

Smart Education Networks that Perform

Marie Bjerede

As school districts embark on digital transformation initiatives, they are recognizing that digital transformation is not an end goal, but rather it is only the beginning. By creating robust technology and human infrastructure, districts are creating not a final end state, but a platform for continual evolution. Technology and education science are in a virtuous spiral which, if allowed, will lead to the ongoing evolution of teaching and learning environments. Internet access, affordable video and content creation and sharing, secure collaboration platforms, and promising (if still immature) digital content have prompted experimentation and shifts in educator practice such as technology-rich project based learning, mastery-based learning and flipped classrooms.

These early technologies have already driven exponential growth in the demand for network capacity and reliability; yet there are even more transformative technologies on the horizon, including innovations in data visualization and dashboards (both third party- and educator-created); embedded digital formative assessment; immersive, adaptive digital content; interoperability infrastructure, and more. There is no end in sight for the co-evolution of technology and education, nor for the demands on education networks and infrastructure.

Once districts commit to digital transformation and begin implementing 1:1 initiatives, the nature of the performance requirements on their infrastructure changes dramatically:

- Capacity demand on education networks increases exponentially every year until maturity.
- Reliability requirements on networks approach "4 nines".

- With open Bring Your Own Device (BYOD) policy, many networks are expected to support three to five student devices with anytime, anywhere access.
- Superintendents are counting on their technology leaders to get high performance networks right in spite of uncertain funding.

District technology leaders are being asked to build and maintain the technology infrastructure required for digital transformation, even as the practice of teaching and learning with technology is rapidly changing and network technology is evolving just as quickly. District leaders are faced with making high-stakes infrastructure investment decisions in an uncertain environment.

Not Just More. Different

The one constant in an uncertain technology landscape is change. And for district leaders the pace of change is accelerating.

For many districts, the Federal Communications Commission's 2017 targets of 1Mbps/student are out of reach. Bandwidth demands are increasing exponentially for most districts that are still on the steep part of the curve, and the jury is still out on where those needs will start to flatten out. To prepare for network growth, it is necessary to build scalable networks that can readily increase their capacity as needed.

Districts that rely on their network infrastructure for instruction report they can really afford no downtime. Zero. These districts are working towards "four nines" of network availability, or less than an hour of unplanned downtime each year.

Most district networks were built to support one computer per staff person, with access primarily to enterprise services. These networks will soon (or may already) be expected to support a device for each student and staff. In BYOD environments, districts are beginning to see three to five devices per user—an increase of two orders of magnitude over the days when districts had, at best, computer labs plus computers for staff. In many districts, users are beginning to expect nearly unlimited robust access to the Internet, 24/7/365 access to digital resources, and many devices will still require secure access to enterprise services both within the building and via external networks.

Traditional school networks generally cannot simply be expanded to meet these needs. They need to be different and (re-)designed holistically. Traditional, occasional, incremental upgrades cannot support the systemic changes that are required to meet the demands of continually evolving education technology utilization and practice.

> In BYOD environments, districts are beginning to see three to five devices per user— an increase of two orders of magnitude over the days when districts had, at best, computer labs plus computers for staff.

To meet the digital challenges of the next few years, districts both small and large must take a holistic approach towards designing their education networks then systematically work towards implementing those designs according to district priorities and financial capacity. This design work is highly complex and involves numerous trade-offs that are often not obvious at first glance. Highly sophisticated districts with professional network architects and engineers are making these trade-offs and pioneering holistic designs. Districts with fewer resources are often looking to professional third party network design vendors or state education and research network services or other consortia to ensure maximum performance and cost efficiency of their infrastructure.

Many elements of smart education network design are counterintuitive in an environment that still thinks of the growth of requirements on the network as linear. The steps below outline considerations that must be intentionally accounted for in the design of smart education networks to ensure that technology investments meet their potential, survive the lifetime of the investment, and do not need to be repeated prematurely due to a failure to recognize the impact of digital transformation on network infrastructure.

Step 1: Set Performance Targets

What network capacity will your district require in five years? How much downtime can your district afford annually, today and five years from now? How many devices are on your district network today, and how many will you support in five years? Although there are no crystal balls, the experience of mature 1:1 implementations and the aggregate

> The key lies in understanding first the realistic initial network usage which requires that stakeholders from across the organization, including the instructional, administrative, and technical areas work together to create a clear vision for what teaching and learning with technology will look like in the district.

experience of districts moving towards digital conversion suggest several rules of thumb for thinking about the growth of network performance requirements.

The key lies in understanding first the realistic initial network usage which requires that stakeholders from across the organization, including the instructional, administrative, and technical areas work together to create a clear vision for what teaching and learning with technology will look like in the district. From this starting point, districts can use the experience of pioneers who are in the trenches of ongoing digital conversion to extrapolate their growing needs over the lifetime of their technology plans.

Step 2: Define Cloud/On-Premise Service Strategy

What data requires high levels of security and where is that best guaranteed? What data needs to be accessed from personal devices via home, cellular or community networks? How scalable and/or redundant does your digital environment need to be? These questions drive decisions regarding the hosting of data, software, and services in individual buildings, district cores, and public or private cloud environments. This in turn drives data flow through the school network and affects capacity and design of the Wide Area Network (WAN). With the current landscape of legislative intervention in issues of data privacy and security, this is no longer simply an issue of cost and quality of solutions for many districts.

Step 3: Investigate Aggregation

For most districts it is difficult to achieve the purchasing power for high capacity networks or the personnel to plan and manage them. There are several aggregation approaches that can give smaller districts the same opportunities as are being implemented by very large districts and states.

Step 4: Design Network

What standards will your network be designed to? Who will design and implement your network? Do you have professional network architecture, design, and engineering expertise in-house, or will you need to consider third party support or managed services? Does your team/ provider have the expertise to design for affordable scalability, high capacity and reliability, anytime/anywhere access, and phased implementation?

Step 5: Evolve Network

Few districts have the resources to implement a high-performance network from scratch. Most districts are faced with evolving their existing networks towards their goals over time. This evolution has three elements: hardware road mapping, capacity scaling, and network monitoring.

First Step: Setting Performance Targets

Surprisingly, building networks to specific performance targets is not the best practice. The reason is that performance needs keep growing, making decisions within a context that assumes performance targets are fixed or even growing linearly, is likely to result in design decisions that aren't sustainable or cost effective over time. And of course, different districts with unique environments will have different performance needs. The best practice is to carefully monitor the network to understand current usage, and to proactively grow capacity, reliability, and device access ahead of the demand curve.

It is not generally until districts begin their digital transformation, moving to transformational environments, that network performance requirements become non-linear. Most districts have gone through an evolution in technology usage, making do with available technology infrastructure that is incrementally improved when needed and when possible. This evolution usually looks like this:

- Basic environments support enterprise systems like student information systems and payroll with staff and educators having access to computers and a computer lab being available for students;

■ Emerging environments support beginning 1:1 efforts;
■ Transformational environments support full 1:1 and/or BYOD;
■ Post-transformational environments evolve to continue to support new usage models and pedagogies as educator practice evolves in response to new technological opportunities.

Districts that are beginning their digital conversion need a starting point, and that starting point is likely to seem so surprisingly large to superintendents, school boards, and bond supporters that it is important to work through the scenarios that the network is expected to support in the near, medium and long term in order to have a context for realistic performance parameter targets.

Four steps will help districts identify general short and medium term performance targets that can be included as network design considerations:

1. Set a starting point based on network usage by existing or planned pilot projects. Perform cross-functional analysis of network demand of planned digital curriculum and resources. In the absence of any other data, plan initially for:
   ■ 100mbps connections as a minimum for all schools;
   ■ Redundant network paths in WAN and to commodity internet;
   ■ Redundant power to network elements that have district-wide effect in case of an outage;
   ■ Addressing and security solutions for one device per student and staff;
   ■ Access to digital resources and tools from external (home and cellular) networks.
2. Extrapolate performance targets for the endpoint of the district technology plan (usually a five year period.)
   ■ Monitor network usage to understand the district-specific growth trends. In the absence of other data for a new implementation, assume network capacity demand will double every 18 months, which means an order of magnitude increase over a five year period.

- ◼ Assume that district reliance on technology for instruction will result in the technology infrastructure becoming mission critical and requiring four or five "nines" availability for network elements that affect the whole district, such as the WAN and Internet connection points.
- ◼ Consider whether the network will be allowed to support one (or as some districts do, three to five) devices per student and staff, as well as guest access for the community.

3. Mitigate the performance requirements as needed. Limiting student access to the Internet to reduce capacity requirements, limiting dependence on technology to reduce reliability requirements, and limiting the need for off-campus access to mitigate digital inequity are all legitimate, though often less than desirable, strategies to balance the goals of technology use with realistic budget constraints.

4. Make purchasing decisions based on the cost cut-off points that will optimize costs over the period of the district technology plan. For example, if the district will require 2Gbps network capacity at the end of the plan, it may make sense to purchase a single 1Gbps router immediately and another after two to three years, whereas if the endpoint is closer to 10Gbps it may be more cost effective to purchase a router with that capacity early.

Setting a Starting Point

Capacity: Districts can estimate initial capacity demands based on the teaching and learning environment the district is implementing. Factors such as the kinds of devices that will be on the network, digital tools and resources to be implemented and policies regarding student devices accessing the network will all contribute to capacity demand.

Reliability: The reliability of the network can be measured as the amount of unplanned downtime that occurs during the year. While in the past districts may be able to tolerate several days per year of unplanned outages, once the shift has been made to transformational environments, districts find it difficult to tolerate even a few hours per year. Some district leaders report that they now need to reduce downtime to less than an hour annually to meet the expectations of their users. Leading districts are:

- Analyzing their district topology and assessing the cost effectiveness of increasing the reliability of their transport layer by moving from star to ring or hybrid topologies, and obtaining secondary Internet connections with distinct up-stream paths;
- Monitoring the health of the network to identify problems;
- Monitoring the capacity demand on the network to stay ahead of the growth curve;
- Monitoring the health of network appliances to minimize downtime for repair/replace/upgrade.

A systematic approach to reliability applies to network transport as well as to network appliances and power. Districts are making cost-benefit tradeoffs by doing careful analysis of the impact of potential outages. A winter storm that takes out power to the district data center and connection to the Internet may be both reasonably likely and highly impactful, making the investment in a secondary data center and/or emergency generator a high priority, while the failure of a single switch or port in a closet may have a small enough impact that redundancy might not be cost effective. Leading districts make tradeoffs based on:

- Probability of failure/outage;
- Impact of outage (number of students affected, expected time to repair or replace);
- Cost of increasing reliability.

Mobility: Designing networks for mobility means:

- Putting in place the infrastructure to support access from personal and/or school devices from home, or via Wi-Fi or cellular data enabled devices from anywhere the students have access to those networks;
- Planning for the MAC and ARP addressing needs of a net-work that supports multiple devices per student (many dis-tricts report they already support three devices per user and expect that to increase);
- Planning cost effective security models for trusted and un-trusted devices;

■ Looking at equity issues for anytime/anywhere ubiquitous access for all students. Districts are designing their networks for this kind of access recognizing that true 24/7/365 ubiquitous access may not be feasible for all students in the short run, but that some student access from home has immediate benefit as the district works towards equitable anytime/anyplace access for all students. In the first stages of implementing anytime/anyplace access, districts can plan for students to access their digital resources and learning communities via home computers and personal devices. As anytime/anyplace demand increases, this will ensure the network architecture is prepared to support it whether through school provided access, student devices, or a hybrid solution that combines both.

Extrapolating Performance Targets

Current performance targets are a snapshot that lies on a curve of ever increasing demand. Districts are seeing exponential growth in demand for capacity as their implementation matures. Although individual district experiences will vary, when looking at large numbers of districts, it is common to see 50-60 percent year over year growth in demand while on the steep part of the growth curve, which implies that if demand needs are being met today, a doubling of capacity every 18 months—a sort of Moore's Law for school networks.

In the early stages of 1:1 implementation, this growth seems to be largely due to additional grade levels or classes being phased into the program. Later, growth can also come from the addition of more devices per student if BYOD policies permit personal devices. In a more mature environment, increased usage of the Internet, additional learning application demand, and novel instructional uses of the devices continue to drive up bandwidth though at perhaps a slower rate. And there is also growth due simply to the increasing size of the resources being accessed via the Internet, such as increased video access and operating system updates.

Districts also need to address the growth in reliability requirements. As instruction comes to depend more and more heavily on Internet access, the district needs to plan for network topologies that are resilient to high impact outages such as cut fiber in the WAN or an outage at their Internet provider.

Finally, districts will need to plan and set policies for the number of student devices and manage the expectations of their community with respect to network access. They should also expect that the fundamental equity issues that divide students with anytime/anywhere access from those without will create increasing pressure to ensure all students have 24/7/365 connectivity, and plan their networks accordingly.

Mitigating Performance Requirements

Capacity mitigating strategies can include:
- Caching technologies;
- Traffic shaping;
- Limiting internet access.

Reliability mitigating strategies can include:
- Contingency planning for outages;
- Less dependence on digital tools and resources.

Mobility mitigating strategies can include:
- Limiting the use of personal devices on the network to reduce addressing requirements;
- Increasing digital equity by working with community to create wireless access opportunities for students at local businesses, restaurants, libraries, or coffee shops;
- Providing access to school Wi-Fi network 24/7.

Making Future-Proofed Purchasing Decisions

To ensure that technology investments are optimized, districts need to build infrastructure that will support the capacity demand of the district for the lifetime of the hardware investment while making prudent financial tradeoffs:
- Identify immediate demand: Districts can identify their immediate demand by carefully monitoring their existing network to understand the usage of pilot programs or current 1:1 classrooms.
- Project future demand: From that starting point, districts should use historical real data from their own network monitoring to understand the growth in demand on your own network if that is available. Think about the demand created

by additional 1:1 learning grade levels or courses that may be added, in what time period. Otherwise use the rule of thumb that demand will double every 18 months.

- Map future demand to investment: Assess whether the hardware investment (fiber, routers, switches, etc.) will support future demand throughout its lifetime.
- Look at price/performance targets: There are specific price cut-offs for networking appliances with, for example 10G appliances being far more expensive than 1G.
- Perform a trade-off analysis to determine whether it is worthwhile to purchase the more expensive high capacity hardware given the expected growth in demand over the next four to seven years.

Second Step: Defining Cloud/On Premise Service Strategy

District decisions regarding where and how to store data, host software, and obtain services will have a significant impact on how much data travels within its WAN and to and from the Internet. This will decide how much WAN capacity and Internet connection capacity will be required to deliver the target capacity goal to each student based on both the amount of data routed inside and outside the Local Area Network (LAN) per student as well as the concurrency factors that apply to that LAN.

Considerations include:

- Legacy systems may still put enterprise and instructional software in school-hosted computers;
- From a technical and tech support perspective, cloud solutions can often be cheaper;
- There is risk that legislation may force districts into maintaining data inside the district rather than taking advantage of these scalable, managed solutions;
- Network needs to be able to support traffic to and from wherever software, apps, and data are stored in addition to the large quantity of Internet traffic.

Third Step: Investigating Aggregation

The Consortium for School Networking's (CoSN's) Infrastructure Survey[1] reports a dramatic difference in the prices different districts pay for Internet access, with some districts paying an unbelievable $800 per Mbps, while 27 percent are able to receive access at $5 or less per Mbps. High costs of internet and high costs of managing and maintaining networks prevent many districts from being able to build out infrastructure at a transformational level.

For many (though not all) districts, there are often aggregation opportunities available that can significantly mitigate these costs, including:

- State research and education networks;
- Purchasing consortia;
- Purchasing and management consortia;
- Third party managed services.

Below are examples of Aggregation Models that have been used or proposed by states and districts:

State-wide Network Aggregates Purchasing and Management of Network to District Internet Connection Point (North Carolina Model)

- A Research and Education Network (REN) provides a state-wide backbone to connect all districts, universities, and colleges.
- The REN connects the backbone to the Internet via multiple providers with discrete upstream routes and uses private peering and Internet2 to minimize traffic across the commodity Internet.
- Each school district connects to the backbone but is responsible for developing its own district WAN as well as the in-building network LAN.
- In North Carolina, the university-based nonprofit Microelectronics Center of North Carolina (MCNC), provides the cost efficiencies of aggregation in many ways.
- MCNC aggregates the funding for statewide core infrastructure that provides a Point of Presence to each district. The

---

[1] http://cosn.org/Infrastructure2016

NCREN backbone connects the points of presence (PoPs) using optical infrastructure with an aggregate capacity of over 160 Gbps.

■ MCNC installs, supports, and manages the state level IT infrastructure.

■ Schools connect to a district hub, usually at a high school or administrative office with 100 Mbps to 1 Gbps connections, and the district hub has a connection to the NCREN backbone provided by state funds and E-Rate. These connections totaled 188 Gbps across 115 districts as of first quarter of 2015.

■ MCNC works with a number of last mile providers to help districts negotiate for their district WAN connections, though the responsibility for this connectivity remains with the district.

Drawbacks: In this model, districts are not required to comply with standards for installing or managing their school infrastructure or WAN, so there is the potential for inconsistency leading to poor designs, planning, or implementation when districts can't afford the network engineering staff to plan and manage their networks.

Potential Variation: Centrally collect E-Rate funds to gain the benefits of aggregating purchases for in-building LAN upgrades or installations or centrally provide guidelines about in-building purchases, installation, and management.

State-wide aggregation of end-to-end network and management (Maine Model)

■ Provide state-wide infrastructure from the device through the Internet connection, including in-building build-out, district WAN's, state backbone, and connection to the Internet.

■ Provide network management and monitoring and network maintenance to the building level.

■ Maine also provides professional development for schools.

Commodity Internet Access Only

■ Instead of a district core, every school goes straight to the Internet through a provider.

■ All district software, services, and data are cloud-based with no district core. All student information is located off-site in the cloud.

Drawbacks: In this model there are no real service guarantees of reliability or bandwidth, school capacity is impacted by other things that are happening in the community that day that eat up bandwidth on the commodity internet. Additionally, many districts are reluctant to place resources in the cloud and believe they can better safeguard private information in a location where they have control of physical security.

Hybrid Model
- Rather than have all the internet traffic at the core of the district or state, there are two paths from each school: one is a VLAN to the district core and one goes directly to commodity internet access.
- Internet access may be via a carrier-neutral data center with a consolidated Internet connection.

This model provides flexibility by supporting a seamless shift of data, software and services between the cloud and a district core.

Aggregation through consortia
- Most consortia aggregate purchasing contracts of hardware and/or Internet access.
- Some consortia aggregate network management services, making high quality network architecture and engineering available to smaller districts who would otherwise be unable to afford them.

Managed Services
- A third-party vendor provides the full infrastructure implementation and subsequent (Day Two) network management in an ongoing basis, 24x7. Equipment and management software lease may be included in the bundle cost. The managed service usually includes a Help Desk functionality for handling issues when they arise.
- This model can make high quality network design and implementation more manageable. It can provide a more consistent cost structure, as multi-year service contracts with pre-determined pricing and payment(s) are involved. Managed services

can off-load existing technology resources from network management duties.

Potential Variation: It is also possible to structured managed services so that equipment is leased rather than purchased, where the periodic upgrading of equipment is negotiated at the end of the term.

Fourth Step: Designing The Network

It is not uncommon for districts to be challenged by the scale and scope of the infrastructure required to support their performance and management requirements. Before beginning network design, districts should consider strategies for mitigating those requirements:

- Consider increasing last-mile access bandwidth by implementing caching technologies rather than or in addition to raw bandwidth upgrades. Although this will not change the requirements on the building LAN or the district WAN, it can reduce the long-term service/bandwidth cost for building access, while increasing network response time. Depending upon the caching design, this can also reduce Internet access upgrade costs.

- Take advantage of purchasing and management aggregation opportunities to reduce the cost of hardware purchases, Internet access and network lifetime management.

For basic and emerging environments, district networks often have legacy systems with comparatively low capacity and reliability. Districts that are not making the shift to digital transformation may not need to make drastic upgrades to their networks. For those moving to transformational environments, however, a holistic design effort that involves all stakeholders in the discussion of requirements and that addresses all aspects of network design collectively in order to make optimal trade-offs, will enable leaders to optimize their technology investments over time.

Holistic design is complex, and requires professional expertise in network architecture and network engineering. For most districts, aggregation strategies such as consortia or third party services that provide network staff across districts is essential to obtain this level of expertise as it is expensive to maintain the needed professionals for just one district.

Comprehensive and Integrated Design Approach

The design of the smart network consists of making tradeoffs and leveraging synergies among multiple interrelated systems. If different design teams evolve an isolated section of the design in a vacuum, the opportunity to leverage opportunities and make those tradeoffs is lost. If, however, the full design of the Smart Education Network is performed holistically, with all elements taken into account, the full cost and performance benefits made possible by current technology and market trends becomes available.

When a methodical approach is applied to designing the optimal network system by examining subsystem design simultaneously, the design outcomes can and should be different. The perfect storm of technology and innovation, policy, funding and the digital revolution and the expectations of a digital society have enabled and demanded this opportunity for an integrated design approach. The comprehensive and integrated design process with the addition of new components into the traditional network architecture is more complex than simply upgrading or expanding existing environment; however, it is a core and foundational approach to redesigning and changing the network to meet the needs of the next five years.

> The comprehensive and integrated design process with the addition of new components into the traditional network architecture is more complex than simply upgrading or expanding existing environment; however, it is a core and foundational approach to redesigning and changing the network to meet the needs of the next five years.

Integrated design demands a purposeful and articulated expectation that the designs of the subsystems will provide more than just interoperability of components. This design must not only meet current needs, but also it must be optimized for advanced functionality and service delivery as the result of the aggregated subsystems' designs and meet the projected needs of the district for the next three to five years.

Every district is different, and how comprehensive design is applied to a given district network will vary. However, there are trade-offs and practices that every district should consider when embarking on a Smart Education Network implementation.

- Begin with a shared vision of the network's purpose. How will it be used today and five years from now? What is the goal for students and how will technology support that? A shared context is critical for making the important trade-offs. Without it, each functional area will optimize for their own sub-system leading to a degradation of the system overall.
- Create a cross-functional team with the job of understanding the infrastructure implications of different decisions regarding the digital environment. For instance:
  - Will the district support BYOD, where the network might be required to support students with three or more devices or will it support 1:1 where the district is responsible for purchasing and managing devices?
  - Will students access their learning community and resources only at school, or at home and places in between?
  - What levels of security and access are required for different software and services?
  - Will the students be using digital curriculum that requires a daily simultaneous download of data to each device?
  - How will teachers be using technology in the classroom and what will their usage patterns look like?
  - What is the financial tradeoff between lower cost Internet appliances with higher bandwidth needs and more expensive devices?
- Take a "greenfield" design mentality. Without the requirements of strategic solutions and greenfield mentality, comprehensive design appears to be the traditional and normal process for design; however, districts must be careful not to fall into the refresh and grow process of existing platforms on an existing network without re-evaluating the overall network design options as they relate to other subsystem needs such as Internet capacity or the application delivery platform. The critical and differentiating component of the Smart Education Network design process is comprehensive and integrated design of the network system as a holistic process. Once a comprehensive design is in place, the implementation can be

staged over many years for optimal cost-effectiveness and budgetary alignment.

- Document the current network design including the Wide Area Network (WAN) and telephone systems and identify alternative providers of services in addition to the traditional vendors:
    - Identify the current information and communication technology infrastructure within your community, region, and state.
    - Identify potential network/fiber providers for your district.
    - Identify the providers of colocation, data center services, and IP access to your community. This may include but not limited to professional Tier 3 or Tier 4 Carrier Neutral Data Centers in the closest metro, the closest termination point of IP Transit Internet services (or Internet Port services, local providers physical service location, and higher education, research, state, and regional networks physical demarcation locations.
- Revisit and update design frequently to respond to the changing environment.
- Mitigate the growing cost of Internet capacity by identifying the optimal physical location for obtaining Internet services. For many districts a Research and Education Network, an intergovernmental cooperative network, or an Internet Point of Presence (PoP) can offer multiple providers as well as virtualized software, storage, and network services. Conduct a cost trade-off between the cost of connecting fiber between the district and such a PoP and the cost reduction available due to eliminating vendor lock-in and reliance on single providers.
- Perform a cost analysis between building, leasing, or otherwise controlling the fiber in your Wide Area Network (WAN) in order to eliminate single-vendor dependence for Internet transport.
- Perform a Total Cost of Ownership analysis between maintaining a physical data center versus remote or virtualized services such as those available at a Carrier Neutral Data Center (CNDC) as a primary data center.

- Mitigate reliability issues by ensuring multiple paths on the WAN, electrical redundancy, and other measures. When making investments evaluate each for redundancy and cost individually. How likely is the failure being mitigated? What is the impact of the failure (single student, classroom, building, district)? How long would it take to repair or route around the failure?
- Consider a Network Function Virtualization Platform (NFV) to support authentication, authorization and accounting for wired and wireless network, active directory, DNS/DHCP, firewall, load-balancing, security and DMZ services. The NFV platform can also support voice IP access services and quality of service. Because the NFV provides a significant amount of East-West traffic, network virtualization should be considered in the overall design for increased security.
- Identify an application delivery strategy—what are the requirements for enterprise, hosted, private/hybrid and public cloud services with respect to access, security, and so on?
- Develop a wide area network infrastructure that is built on a design that provides scalability, capacity, high availability and ease of management including an internal network transport layout (discussed below), an external connection options, estimated cost of POP co-location, Internet cost and options and PSTN cost and option. Also, identify access to peering and/or state network services to augment the commodity Internet service.

In the majority of cases, a high level design with the Smart Education Network strategy Internet and Internet Provider services requirements and design solutions of the cost efficiencies and scalability alone will validate the need for the new network design architecture. However, when the other service requirements for PSTN access, application delivery platform, network/data center solutions, disaster recovery/business continuity and cloud services are considered through a comprehensive and integrated design process, the new network design infrastructure solution will clearly show both the immediate and long term strategic value to the district.

Note that for those districts where it is cost effective, moving their Internet access and data center to a PoP is the prime enabler for numerous cost efficiencies and improvements in ease of management, reliability and scalability. For small districts or districts that are highly geographically distributed, this approach may not be the most cost-effective. Each district must make those trade-offs holistically and independently.

Also note that these steps do not address the issue of human capacity for network architecture and management. For many districts it may be more cost effective, reliable, and sustainable to contract network design, build-out, and maintenance from a third party with service level agreements and built-in technology refresh than to compete with industry for highly qualified network specialists.

Step Five: Evolve Network

Few districts have the resources to implement a high-performance network from scratch. Most districts are faced with evolving their existing networks towards their goals over time. This evolution has three elements: hardware road mapping, capacity scaling, and network monitoring.

Hardware Road Mapping

Often, the holistic network design of a smart network will call for significant upgrades to existing networks such additional fiber for creating a more resilient network topology; shifts in data storage, software hosting, and services away from a single district core; and multiple upstream routes to the commodity Internet. However, these infrastructure upgrades that increase network performance can still be ineffectual from the student device perspective if in-building upgrades that support the capacity demands are not also in place. All it takes is one bottleneck such as inadequate capacity through the access points, slow transport from the access point to the closet, or low capacity switches, to make the student experience continue to be slow and inadequate.

> Infrastructure upgrades that increase network performance can still be ineffectual from the student device perspective if in-building upgrades that support the capacity demands are not also in place.

Upgrade roadmaps should prioritize:

- Making investments that move towards the new network design;
- Maximizing the improvement of the user experience given the resources available.

Capacity Scaling

The most cost effective way to increase capacity at need is to purchase services that allow the district to pay only for capacity that is actually used, and to increase capacity by simply requesting a new level of service without requiring any hardware upgrades. When available, districts can purchase these kinds of service for Internet access, cloud-based network functionality (such as content filters), and data storage and software hosting.

Network Monitoring

By monitoring the network, districts can proactively scale the capacity provided while maintaining uptime and reliability. Districts can:

- Monitor capacity to ensure that peak usage doesn't increase over 65 percent utilization;
- Monitor congestion to address issues with network configuration;
- Monitor performance of appliances to ensure proactive and timely replacement of failing components.

A Demanding and Uncertain Future

Smart education networks not only meet the current demands, but are flexible and scalable enough to cost-effectively grow as those demands increase. Where the exponential growth that districts see in their 1:1 initiatives will level out is unknown, and will vary from district to district. By designing smart networks with a scalable architecture, districts can keep up with the technology requirements of evolving instructional approaches and the growing availability of digital tools and resources.

MARIE BJEREDE, *an established authority on mobile learning, is Principal for Mobile Learning and Infrastructure at the Consortium for School Networking (CoSN), the Founder of e-Mergents LLC, and a 25-year veteran executive leader in high-tech and wireless communication development. Bjerede advises schools, startups, and technology leaders on the products, practices, and platforms that enable and scale authentic learning and teaching with technology. Bjerede takes an unconventional approach in all her endeavors—removing constraints from systems to get bigger payoffs with less effort.*

Prior to her work in education, Bjerede worked in high-tech product development and executive leadership, leading teams of hundreds of engineers in developing cutting-edge communications products. She also spent over a decade as Vice President and General Manager for Qualcomm's Portland Design Center, a cross-disciplinary center of excellence.

7

A Question for the New Technology Leader: Developing the Case for Greater IT Investments

Dennis Fazio

After the evening's community info session, a technology referendum voter approaches. "What can we really expect from this expense? You bought all those Smart Boards a while back, and my kid didn't seem any smarter than if you just used a blackboard." At a board presentation, a business executive on your school board interrupts: "What's the return on investment (ROI) on this $360,000 network upgrade? How do we know what all this technology stuff, that you now want to add here, is really costing us?" In your budget meeting, your superintendent chimes in: "So what are all the hidden costs of this new student database system? How much is this going to continue costing us down the road?"

Your district finally saw the light, and put a Chief Technology Officer in place—you. In your second year, you are desperate to move ahead with key technology updates and upgrades to, first of all, keep things afloat, and then to move the district into the modern era with proven educational technology and its supporting infrastructure. Can you answer these questions well enough to win over the voter, respond to your board member, and reassure your superintendent? If you can't, your whole technology program is at risk, and you can probably kiss both your ambitions and control of your budget goodbye, because others will cut them down to size.

How can you explain the supposed improvements this referendum will provide? How do you speak in the business terms your board wants to hear to justify your big hit on the capital budget? How do you make the rest of your district cabinet understand the true total cost and benefits of these educational technology investments?

You do it by removing from their minds the concept that educational technology is an expense or cost center. You present that this is an investment; one that will provide clear justifiable value—the *value of investment*. You must argue that though some investments will provide financial return in long-term *quantitative* cost or efficiency (ROI), most of the results will be in the realm of *qualitative* value—an improvement in student learning, and a way to reach the strategic goals of the district. You also show you have the complete financial and strategic story because you've accounted for all the short-term and long-term costs, direct and indirect, that will accrue over the years—the *total cost of ownership*. Value return and total cost explained in clear strategic terms with real numbers; no hand waving or vague platitudes.

Smart Investments in Information Technology

As states and school districts better recognize the need for a robust technology infrastructure for digital learning and assessment initiatives, tight budgets are weighed against overall cost savings afforded by increasingly workable technologies. Nonetheless, the focus on near-term solutions to patch immediate needs and some skepticism on the efficacy of educational technology makes effective implementation and support of large technology deployments increasingly difficult. Schools often operate by making short-term decisions without fully evaluating implementation challenges and long-term effects. Many districts simply delay replacements or defer maintenance—not a smart move when changing the culture of teaching and learning is also a top desire.

Consortium-School Networking's (CoSN) SmartIT initiative provides strategic recommendations for the smart Chief Technology Officer (CTO). There are several smart ways to address the cost and choices of technology infrastructure and projects. SmartIT addresses these with a strategy of applying interactive tools to tie the district's technology investments to its strategic goals. Your district can keep your technology programs intact, and position itself to run a smarter, stronger, and more cost-effective technology—and education—operation.

What is SmartIT?

SmartIT is an initiative to help Chief Technology Officers/district technology leaders, superintendents and budget officers master tight budgets, and effectively support educational needs with appropriate strategic decisions in technology investments. School technology programs and replacement cycles—with all the proven benefits they offer to educators and students—are often underfunded. Such constraints present not just challenges, but also opportunities to rethink and strengthen technology investments, operations, programs, plans, staff and results. SmartIT will help technology leaders move forward in key areas with tools and resources that enlighten and guide your efforts in a way that makes sense for your circumstances and strategic goals.

Return on Investment, Value of Investment, Total Cost of Ownership

Your board chair states, "Businesses has to show the return on investment for technology, why can't our district?" Believe it or not, this is an increasingly common question, and one with some legitimacy in light

The **SmartIT Initiative** reflects the ongoing priority for technology leaders to strategically plan and manage IT investments by providing tools and resources that focus on:

- **Student outcomes and budget management:** Making technology core to the teaching and learning mission to increase student achievement even as budgets shrink.

- **Total cost of ownership:** Understanding the direct and indirect costs of implementing and maintaining computing devices and related infrastructure, and using those costs to articulate the effects of proposed changes and to reduce operational costs.

- **Value of investment:** Evaluating proposed projects through cost-benefit analysis to understand and articulate the financial and non-financial benefits of projects in terms that allow stakeholders to understand the value of the investment.

Figure 7-1. SmartIT Initiative

of some reports of lack of real educational achievement from previous expensive technology expenses in computers.

So, how do you even begin to answer your school board chair; how does the savvy Chief Technology Officer demonstrate the technology project is worth the investment? In schools, the discussion should be around *value of investment* (VOI) as a more appropriate value than return on investment—a business term calculated by measuring benefits in dollars to the top or bottom line of the business. Our public schools are not profit-driven entities, and do not measure their success in financial terms. The business of schools is child development and learning. School system leaders must understand their district's educational goals, and how technology will support those goals. They need to demonstrate the *value* of the technology investment.

Now, there are occasions when a large investment can be shown to save overall expense or improve operational efficiency in the current educational program. With those technology projects, leaders then need to demonstrate a business-focused return on investment.

Most importantly, it is not adequate to only deal with the initial investment, though that is the most visible focus of a large capital investment, sometimes purchased with levy dollars. The operational and support costs over the life of the investment are just as important and can often add up to be larger than the initial purchase and installation. To account for that, technology leaders must make the *project total cost of ownership* (Project TCO) a major part of their planning and investment decisions.

Likewise, when annual budgets are developed, there is a tendency to cut from administrative programs to provide funding for classroom activities. Unfortunately, cuts in information technology funding (such as delaying replacement cycles or reducing IT personnel) often lead to increased expenses for the school system in terms of computer downtime and end user time dealing with technology issues. It is in the best interest of the school system for leaders to understand the ramifications of technology budget cuts in terms of *the entire IT environment total cost of ownership* (TCO).

The Two Key Resources for SmartIT

CoSN's SmartIT resources are provided in two areas to put technology investments in perspective:

1. **TCO assessment tools**

   A Total Cost of Ownership Assessment can be a holistic approach to understanding costs and effects of cuts. These TCO assessment tools are focused on the district's *entire IT environment* as opposed to focusing on *a specific project.* TCO is a methodology to measure and understand all of the costs of acquiring and maintaining the district's entire IT infrastructure and operations including all infrastructure, user hardware and software, staff support costs and user-related costs. A TCO assessment will help you articulate in quantifiable terms the overall effects to the district of proposed budget cuts or other changes that could actually result in inefficiencies. For instance, cutting a technical support staffer may look good on paper, but that person's work doesn't just go away; it shifts to teachers or other support staff who may be expensive and not adequately trained to fix computer and network problems. The net result is frustration, inadequate lesson planning, unavailable lab systems and slow resolution to administrative system problems. A good TCO assessment will empower district leaders to make informed decisions about the effects of reducing support staff or delaying needed hardware and software upgrades.

2. **VOI project tools**

   The VOI Project Benefits Workbook and VOI Project Cost Estimator Workbook comprise the VOI Project Tools. These are focused on *a specific project* as opposed to focusing on the district's *entire IT operations.* The VOI project tools are designed to help school leaders measure the costs and benefits—both tangible and intangible—of proposed projects and connect these benefits to the organization's mission, goals, and mandates. For projects focused on saving money only, the VOI Project Cost Estimator also provides a Return on Investment (ROI) calculator and payback time.

Knowing Your Total Cost of Ownership

TCO is a comprehensive way to understand all of the costs involved in implementing and maintaining technology in the school system. Direct costs include technology (hardware, including network infrastructure, software, and external service providers) and labor (both IT department and any other district or contracted personnel responsible for supporting the technology infrastructure). But TCO also takes into account unbudgeted indirect costs, which are the costs of user time in technology training and dealing with technology issues.

Performing a total cost of ownership assessment takes time, effort and input from other departments. So, why go through this process?

- TCO is a valuable tool in the budgeting process. With a TCO assessment you can model the effects of proposed IT personnel changes or delayed technology upgrades.
- Annual assessments allow you to continually measure and compare progress towards a more efficient technology environment, including both direct and indirect costs.
- TCO provides insight into value of investment costs (VOI project TCO) for proposed technology related projects, helping to ensure appropriate resources for project implementation and ongoing support.

With SmartIT, CoSN firmly believes it is possible and important to understand all of the costs involved in implementing and maintaining your technology infrastructure. We have constructed an Excel workbook tools and user survey to do so. The TCO assessment workbook and the end user survey for indirect labor for input to the TCO assessment workbook are available on the TCO section of the CoSN SmartIT web site.

Total Cost of Ownership Tips and Recommendations

1. **Get executive support.**
   A TCO assessment includes time to gather input and analyze the results. It requires cooperation from other departments including HR or payroll and the business office. Executive support is important to raise the level of awareness and to compel participation and buy-in from other departments.

2. **Use a baseline.**
   To understand current baseline costs, conduct an enterprise-wide study of your current year costs. This can then be used for comparison scenarios or subset studies.

3. **Survey users for indirect labor.**
   The best way to determine the indirect labor components (time spent by users in training or dealing with computer related issues) is to survey a statistically significant subset of users. Since it will take a couple of weeks to get the results back, it helps to get the survey out early. Surveying students is optional, but teachers, aides, and administrative staff should be surveyed. The TCO tool is looking for the total number of indirect labor hours, not an average. Use the downloaded Indirect Labor User Survey to assemble this data. You can then easily copy and paste in one action the results of each returned survey into the TCO workbook.

4. **Make educated estimates.**
   TCO is not an exact science. A good educated estimate for any input field with some limited research is adequate; over time your processes and accuracy will improve. For instance, to obtain the amortized cost for client computers purchased over the last four or five years, you don't need to pull all of those invoices. If you know how many client computers you have bought over that time period and about what they cost on average, you have a good estimate.

5. **Include all direct labor.**
   Direct labor includes all personnel who have at least a part-time responsibility for supporting the computing environment, measured in full-time equivalents (FTE). This may include teachers, school personnel who are not part of the district computer services organization, outsourced services, and no-cost students and volunteers. Understanding this direct labor allocation will allow you to evaluate the most efficient approach to support. Note that technology education teachers should not be included unless part of their time (pay) is designated to technology support.

6. **Include as much data as possible.**
   Depreciate major software purchases (initial licenses) and

include annual licensing fees. Contracted labor services, such as hardware maintenance contracts, can be included under Direct Labor/Outsourced. Internet service providers and other external services go under Technology/Other/External Application Providers.

7. **Use the example workbook.**
    An example workbook completed with sample values to give you some guidance in completing your Assessment is available on the TCO section of the CoSN SmartIT web site.

The CoSN Value of Investment Methodology

But, how do you then measure investments in technology that are focused on educationally critical, yet qualitative benefits? For example, most school districts have a long-range strategic plan with goals like:

- Increasing student achievement;
- Increasing student engagement;
- Improving attendance and behavior;
- Attracting and retaining staff;
- Developing 21st century skills for students;
- Decreasing drop-out rates for at-risk students;
- Engaging parents and communities.

With SmartIT, CoSN firmly believes it is possible and important to measure qualitative benefits in addition to quantitative benefits. We have constructed two Excel workbook tools to do so on the VOI section of the SmartIT web site.

This approach can be used to:

- Sell a project internally or to the School Board;
- Articulate the costs and benefits of the project to constituents;
- Evaluate the comparative costs and benefits of two or more projects competing for the same funding;
- Determine later whether a project should be sustained.

The steps to follow when performing a project-based Value of Investment exercise include:

1. **Determine cost.**
    The first step is to understand the cost of the technology initiative over the life of the *project*—the project Total Cost of Ownership (Project TCO). The concept behind TCO, as mentioned,

is to determine all of the costs involved in securing and operating the proposed project.

Initial purchases, training and implementation costs must be amortized or annualized, and ongoing costs must be included. For example, to do this for a projected 1:1 initiative, initial amortized costs could include devices over four years, yearly network upgrades for broadband capacity, and initial teacher training over four years. Unbudgeted but real costs include indirect labor, which is the hidden cost of time spent by users in training and handling technology problems. Typically, these unbudgeted costs are as large as or even larger than the direct costs. A Project Cost Estimator to help you identify and summarize all of these costs is available on the VOI section of the SmartIT web site.

2. **Calculate anticipated savings and revenues.**

   Most projects, even those focused on qualitative benefits such as student achievement, have some cost savings. There may also be some anticipated increase of revenues based on higher attendance, grants, or state/federal aid. The Project Cost Estimator allows you to identify and apply infrastructure and support savings to the project cost, and the VOI Project Benefits Workbook will help you identify other dollar savings, user productivity enhancements and increased revenue, and apply them as benefits. Qualitative benefits, such as student achievement or the political value of increasing community support, should be stated in measurable terms as completely as possible.

   > Most projects, even those focused on qualitative benefits such as student achievement, have some cost savings.

   Important note: The remaining steps in this process must be done as a team effort, and not just by the Chief Technology Officer or technology leader. This involves judgements regarding the district's strategic goals, their relative importance and the assignment of quantitative values to the qualitative goals. This requires the participation of and consensus of key district strategic leaders, including the superintendent (or assistant superintendent), the Chief Financial Officer or business manager, and perhaps even the curriculum director, along with any others on the strategic team.

3. Measure (score) "qualitative" benefits.
Since the business of schools is education, and schools operate for the public good, many or most of the benefits of implementing technology cannot be measured in terms of dollars; we call these qualitative benefits. For these to be considered benefits they must directly or indirectly affect the school or district strategic plan—mission, goals and mandates. A VOI Project Benefits workbook is provided on the VOI section of the SmartIT web site to help you to identify and apply these qualitative benefits with the following:
   a. Determine school/district goals and assign a relative importance to each.
   b. Align anticipated project benefits with the appropriate goals.
   c. State the anticipated project benefits in measurable terms.
   d. Agree on the effect of each benefit on applicable goals; a total qualitative benefits score is calculated.
   e. Enter probability of success; the total qualitative score is multiplied by the probability of success for a risk-weighted benefits score.
Figure 7-2 shows an example of the result of this process.

4. Compare projects
For each project you now have a cost and a benefits score. A higher score indicates a bigger project benefit. So for each project, Score ÷ Cost = Bang-for-the-Buck. The project with the highest Bang-for-the-Buck provides the most value for the expenditure.

5. Evaluate results.
Once your project has been implemented, you have an opportunity to objectively review actual costs and benefits versus the projected costs and benefits. This will allow you to concisely

respond to the project skeptics. Since the anticipated costs and benefits were stated in measurable terms, the actual results can be measured:

    a. Actual costs vs. anticipated costs;

    b. Actual savings or revenues vs. anticipated savings revenue;

    c. Actual measurable benefits vs. anticipated benefits.

School or District Mission, Goals and Mandates	Importance 1 - 10	Anticipated Project Benefits* State in Measurable Terms (Substitute your specific project goals)	Effect* -10 to +10	Score (Calculated)	$ Savings
Perform within top 25% of schools in the state	7.0	Raise one-to-one student math scores from 57% passing to 62% passing by 2011	4	28	
		Raise one-to-one student language arts scores from 55% passing to 62% passing by 2011	3	21	
Keep students in school through graduation	5.0	Increase graduation rate from 87% to 94% for this graduating in 2011	9	45	
Prepare students for workforce and college success	8.0	90% of students will graduate with measured proficiency in the following 21st century skills by 2013: Teamwork and collaboration (imbeded in social studies core) Higher order thinking (imbeded in math and science core) Communication and presentation (imbeded in social studies and language arts core)	5	40	
Provide equal opportunity for all students	9.0	Each student will have 24/7 access to a computer, software image and internet	3	27	
		Gap on standardized math for minorities will close from 8% to 4% by 2011	2	18	
		Dropout rate for minority students will decrease from18% to 8% by 2012	2	18	
		Close gap on standardized test scores for students wit disabilitie from 8% to 3% by 2012	1	9	
		Total Score and Dollar Value for this Project		206	$0
Probability of Success	90%	**Risk-weighted Dollar Value and Score for this Project**		175	$0

Figure 7-2. Project Benefits table

Total Cost of Ownership Methodology Flowchart

The flow for executing the VOI methodology is shown in Figure 7-3 (see next page).

The Bottom Line

Understanding the costs and assessing the value of a district's IT environment and any proposed technology projects is vital if you, the technology leader, want to have credibility with your school board, CFO, superintendent, and community. Clearly it takes work even with the CoSN tools. But, the reward in doing this is a concise understanding of the projected benefits and informed decision-making, and the ability to answer your school board and community when asked about the technology investment.

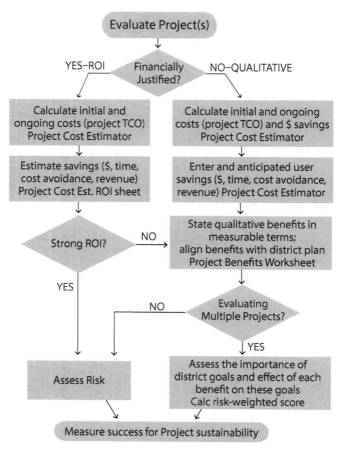

Figure 7-3. Flow for executing the VOI methodology

DENNIS FAZIO *is an electrical engineer who started out by designing supercomputers before that industry was waylaid by the microprocessor, and rooms full of equipment moved to a box by your deskside and then to your pocket. He then moved on to the Internet when it was just a sparse bundle of academic networks, and built a statewide Internet organization covering most of the major businesses and colleges in Minnesota. After a stint in enterprise architecture for the state government, he again built an Internet service and technology consulting team within a public Ed Tech organization, this time for school districts covering about 40 percent of the students in the state. He now has eased off to part-time activities in educational technology systems and community organizing in the Twin Cities of Minnesota.*

8

The Process of Change in Education

Greg Mathison Jr., Ed.D.
Stephen Hankins, Ed.D.

The word "process" is usually not welcomed by leaders. A process involves slowing down and taking time to systematically break down a situation to determine the correct course of action. Leaders often prefer to dictate change from above. They feel it is their duty and right, due to their position, to create a vision and goals for the people they lead, and then delegate the work to accomplish those goals to other leaders within the organization. Dictating change is more time efficient and controllable; the outcomes are predictable giving a "you do this, you get that" model.

This type of process may work in organizations that are measured by profit margins. However, it does not work in education. To spark change in education, there needs to be a buy-in from all the stakeholders involved. An established culture of innovation and

> To spark change in education, there needs to be a buy-in from all the stakeholders involved.

trust must be present. The change must be part of the culture unless it is the culture you are trying to change. Students, teachers, parents, support staff, and the community a school serves, all need to believe in what the school stands for. The evidence of a successful education is not test scores alone. It also includes the social-emotional development of each student. In order to meet the needs of students, school must not only successfully teach content, but it must also support and develop self-confident and self-motivated, lifelong learners. To accomplish this, all stakeholders must feel they are a part of something bigger than themselves; that the school has a moral purpose, not just a bottom line measured by standardized test scores.

The process of change/innovation is messy. It takes time, a willingness to explore costs and benefits, and the institutional freedom to implement the proposed change. The more people actively involved in the process, the greater chance that the outcome will create a unified vision and be sustainable long term. This can be scary as the change may not be exactly what was anticipated from the start. So, where do you start? First, creating change in education starts with the community agreeing on what it values. Identifying a school's shared core values is like laying down railroad tracks. The tracks are the guides that will lead the locomotive to its destination. If the tracks are not properly placed, the train will derail, and cause a lot of damage. The success of any change is dependent on the rails that are put in place.

> Creating change in education starts with the community agreeing on what it values.

Identifying shared values is a crucial rail that takes work and time to create. Stakeholders need an opportunity to voice their beliefs and feel that their input has been taken into account. Surveys, open houses, casual conversation in the halls during parent-teacher conferences, focus groups that include students, parents, teachers, support staff, and community leaders are all necessary to discover those values. A school leader needs to ask the community what its core values are, and then ask "What do you want your school to look like in five years?" Conversations with the community should focus on identifying core values and establishing a moral imperative. The members of a school community need to feel connected to the process, and the outcomes of that process should represent their wishes and desires to provide the best possible educational experience for their children. When a leader can tap into the core of what motivates and excites the people he or she leads, significant and lasting change can be made.

Creating a culture in which continual improvement is the expectation, not the exception, requires a simple vision that everyone can understand and follow. Having a trusting and safe work environment is also critical. A great example of a simple and powerful shared vision comes from the Massai tribe. They live their lives focused on one question: "How are the children?" If the answer is not "All the children are well", then it is a moral imperative to make the necessary changes to ensure that every child is well. A very simple question can lead to action and a powerful common vision. Schools need a vision that is simple but powerful. There is power in having a vision that is general enough that each person can personalize what that vision means to him or her individually. Asking a guiding question to help mold the vision for a school promotes empowered conversations among the staff. The question should not have a "correct" answer, but should be worded in a way that makes everyone's answer valid. People need to feel their voice/opinion is worthy of consideration. and that builds trust.

Trust is necessary to make meaningful change and promote innovation in the classroom. Building trust with a staff takes time. Relationships must be built and tested before a staff will move.

Simon Sineck, in his book *Leaders Eat Last,* makes an excellent point about staff needing to trust their leader to feel safe in their work environment. Sinek continues to explain that leaders need to create a culture where people support one another. A leader needs to eliminate all internal threats. There are plenty of external issues that a school deals with each day. Staff members need to know that they are valued and part of a family. If teachers feel that they have a supportive leader, and the people around them value who they are, they will be willing to take risks. Change in education needs teachers to take risks, to try new things to meet the needs of their students without fear of what will happen to them from within. Trust is developed one conversation and one interaction at a time. It is developed through empowering staff and trusting their professionalism to make decisions focused on kids. Dr. Terry Adams, a retired superintendent, stated, "You cannot lead people you don't know." The true educational leaders aren't confined to the office or meetings; they are out in the halls and classrooms. They must know their staff and students as their own family. True and lasting change cannot be generated from the top down.

> Change in education needs teachers to take risks, to try new things to meet the needs of their students without fear of what will happen to them from within.

Educational leaders needs to lead not manage. They need to see the big picture when creating change. They must be aware of the ripple effect that may result from the change; but must not let fear of the ripple effect keep them from making taking those chances. The process of successful change in education is dependent on having leaders that focus on people, and are willing to take chances. The implementation of that change is dependent on the people who are being led to manage and carry out the changes. Building trust and eliminating the threats from within take time and strong leadership. It is the only way to make meaningful and lasting change in education. The difficult part for a leader is how to measure and determine if they have created that culture in their building. Making small changes that have a strong chance to be successful, is a good way for a leader to get a feel of the climate in their building as well as helping to build trust among the community. YB Yates stated, "Education is not the filling of a pail, but a lighting of a fire." This is what makes change in education so exciting and so difficult at the same time. Innovation and change in education do not result from completing a series of tasks/goals on a list created by the state to measure a school's effectiveness. Too often, the same criteria used to encourage and promote success in all schools results in schools using the same cookie-cutter program. Change in education usually occurs because one school or school district innovated and created a new system to meet the challenge/standards of new state testing and/or requirements. Other districts want to have the same success so they copy as best they can exactly what the successful school/school district is doing. Although the changes the districts make are based on data and are often good changes, there are problems created that can inhibit true innovation and change.

First, the change being prescribed is top-down. There is no ownership from the teachers or school community. Often, a school will bring in an expert on a newest program and spend thousands of dollars on professional development to implement it. Teachers are then asked to go and implement the new program in their classroom, without having

> Making small changes that have a strong chance to be successful, is a good way for a leader to get a feel of the climate in their building as well as helping to build trust among the community.

been asked for input. Teachers are often fearful to experiment with the new program or still do not have enough knowledge about it to be able to adapt it to their classroom. The second problem is the "this too shall pass" attitude. Experienced educators have seen multiple changes in education over time. Often, the newest way of teaching is just an old method with a new name.

They may choose to wait it out, and do enough of whatever new expectation is being required of them to keep the boss happy. The result of this is that those teachers spend their energy on trying to keep the things the same instead of trying to look for how the new program can add to their teaching repertoire.

A school leader that creates a culture of trust and respect will have drastically different results implementing the same program from a similar school leader that does not. The school that eliminates the inside threats and challenges teachers to take risks will create lasting and impactful change. Teachers who are "commissioned to go and innovate" will seek out the newest program and research and make it their own. It is up to the leader to "light the fire." "Lighting the fire" is creating a culture in which teachers look at the latest research and methodology as an opportunity, not as something else they must drop in their bucket.

Bottom line, to be successful, lasting change and innovation are grassroots movements. Great leaders empower teachers to innovate and take risks to reach their student's needs. Leaders help the early adopters get the support they need to be successful via encouragement, professional development, and freedom to take educational risks. The change becomes contagious as teachers see other teachers having success with new ideas. When teachers lead the change, it is internalized by the institution; change from the inside out is the most impactful change. The leader creates the environment that supports and promotes the positive changes within the building by pouring faith and resources to those that have the most impact on our children, the teachers.

> When teachers lead the change, it is internalized by the institution; change from the inside out is the most impactful change.

DR. GREG MATHISON, *Jr. has served as Head Principal of Marquette High School in the Rockwood School district for seven years (St. Louis, MO). He started his career eighteen years ago as a high school mathematics teacher and coach (football, basketball, and baseball). Greg enjoys spending time with his family (Linda, Lexi, Mikaela, and Riley) when he isn't attending a Marquette event.*

DR. STEPHEN HANKINS *is the Associate Principal at Marquette High School in Chesterfield, Missouri. This is his twentieth year in education. He is happily married to Melissa, and they have four beautiful children (Abigail, Hannah, Madison and Raegan).*

9

Reinventing School: Vision and Planning for Technology in Education

James G. Lengel

Why Vision and Planning?

This chapter is designed to help you lead a school to reinvent itself to take full advantage of digital technologies for teaching and learning. It is based on the experience of dozens of schools and districts, and illustrated with examples from Denver, Colorado, and Rochester, New York. These districts mounted collaborative efforts to reinvent themselves by imagining what a day in the life of a student should look like, publishing this vision to the community, and then using it as a source for planning and implementation.

The chapter begins with a rationale for vision and planning, includes samples from the work at Denver and Rochester, and closes with step-by-step suggestions for you to follow as you lead a similar effort in your own district.

Why Should You Do This?
Shared Understanding
Perhaps the many actors involved in education and technology in your school or district need to move toward a consensus among the many ongoing projects and pilots in this area. Perhaps you need to develop a consistent understanding—internally among staff and leadership—of the value of technology in education. Perhaps you need to help your information technology folks see the real benefits of technology to students, and understand their personal link to the work of students.

Perhaps you need to unite a disparate leadership team in your city. The visioning process described in this chapter can help move forward on all of these fronts.

Community Support

Perhaps you need a clear picture of the benefits of technology in schools to build support in the community, among citizens, taxpayers, parents, and policy-makers. Perhaps you need to generate enthusiasm and buy-in for your technology efforts. Perhaps a compelling vision can serve as a precursor to raising the funds necessary to moving forward.

Collaboration

The visioning process described here and followed by many schools and districts around the world is based on collaboration. The visions were created not by charismatic leaders or visionary vendors or geeky technicians, but by the students, teachers, and principals who work in the schools. It's a user-centric approach. The value of collaboration among the small groups that brainstormed scenes for the *Day-in-the-Life,* and the sharing across groups of these dreams, formed the essential core of the process.

The relationships built during the visiting process—between the IT folks and the instructional leadership, between the teachers and the technical staff, and among all levels of the school community—have served to enable progress even in difficult times. Most schools have found that the process of reinvention brought people together and helped them transform very conservative institutions.

How Is It Done?

More than 30 schools and districts across the world followed a similar process to reinvent themselves:

1. They recruited and selected a cross-functional, **representative group** that included teachers, students, principals, parents, IT staff, vendors, and community members.
2. In small, mixed groups, these collaborators **sketched scenes** of a day in the life of a student using technology for learning.
3. They **shared and discussed** these sketches across groups and across communities.

4. They remained focused throughout on the **student point of view:** what the student was actually doing as he or she used technology for learning.
5. They combined the sketches and scenes into a **narrative story**—a script—with human and dramatic appeal.
6. They developed the script into **video** that helped make the vision concrete and specific for the broader community of leaders, teachers, students, and community members.

Two Illustrations

The result of this reinvention process can be seen in these two examples of *A Day in the Life of a Student* from Denver and Rochester. The development and distribution of this *Day in the Life* story is the centerpiece of the process.

DAY IN THE LIFE: DENVER

What would a day in the life of a Denver student look like if we took full advantage of the possibilities of the new technologies for teaching and learning? The text and video link below follow some students through such a day.

Let Alex and Maya, two Denver students, describe a day in their lives in their reinvented schools.

Connections

Alex: Connections make the world work. And learning is all about making connections that are meaningful to me. More than ever before, technology can personalize my education, and help me make those connections.

Maya: How will we build these connections, and the potential for making new ones? What will my learning in a connected Denver Public Schools look like?

Alex: My name is Alex. I'm ten years old and in 5th grade. My mom drops me off at school on her way to work. While I eat breakfast, I look at the Student Portal. I can see my schedule for the day and what I'll be working on in each of my classes.

Connecting Activity

Maya: I'm Maya. I'm 15, in 11th grade, but I'm taking AP Calculus and a college course, too. Before I even leave for school in the morning, I check in using the Student Portal. I start choosing from my day's suggested lessons and activities. My deadlines are all laid out for me. And I can tell my advisor that I'll drop by her office when I get to school.

Connecting Concepts

Alex: In Math, we start with adding and subtracting fractions with different denominators. My favorite part is that I get to choose how I show what I am learning. Our teacher shows some of us on the interactive whiteboard, while a few of us already know how. We follow along on our tablets, or tap on some of the links for extra help. It is easy to learn more when everything is just a tap away.

Connecting Students

Alex: We break into small groups. Ms. Foster knows who goes together because of the information she gets from her computer. The groups change all the time, based on what we need. But, we can get help from other groups or from Ms. Foster, just by asking a question from our tablet.

Connecting to the world

Maya: In the economics unit that I selected, we're working on a project with some students in Lima, Peru, studying the path of copper from the mines in Peru to its use here in the United States. We have meetings over video chat. We're collecting information, and creating a script together that will eventually turn into a short documentary video. And we're able to do this as a group, even though we're 4,000 miles away from one another.

Connecting to the Earth

Alex: We have a school garden that provides some of the vegetables for our cafeteria. It's my job to track these vegetables in our online spreadsheet. How many we harvest, how many are eaten, how much is thrown away. The information automatically goes to some high school students who are collecting this information from schools all over town. Then we're showing how growing our own food compares to schools where they buy all of it.

Connecting to Nature
Maya: School is the hub for my learning, but it's not the only place I learn. No matter where I am, I can check in on the resources that my teachers provide, stay in touch with my teachers, or connect to my friends for help. And I can help them too.

Connecting to Community
Maya: My internship is at a water policy organization this semester. I got to go out and do testing of ground water. I helped the engineers collate and present the data. My work counted toward mastery of many state standards and credit in chemistry and my journalism class.

Connecting Language
Alex: When I moved to the U.S., I didn't speak English. I'm still not great at writing it. But, I can translate or look things up on my tablet when I need to. Ms. Santistevan has us publish our best pieces on the class site. When I know others can see my work, it makes me try really hard. Ms. Santistevan says that hard work has shown in my class projects and in my test scores.

Connecting School with the World
Maya: My Mandarin class is all online. I access the lessons, join conversation groups, and record and turn in all my work online. This lets me take the class when I want, so I can fit in things like the internship. And it lets us pick some classes that only two or three of us might have taken.

Connecting Body and Mind
Alex: I don't spend the whole day doing school work. After school, I have soccer. I'm sure the adults think we're learning something, but we all just like to have fun together.

Connecting Families with School
Alex: When my mom and I both get home, she can help me with my homework. She can see everything that is due, and get links to

directions that show her how to help me. I am proud of my portfolio, and she can see my work.

Maya: My mom travels for work a lot. It's pretty easy for her to stay in touch with dad and me.

Mom: I set up alerts, and send mom updates so she can stay in touch with my schoolwork, too. She gets to see all the same cool things dad and I can see, including how I'm doing. She gets to hear from my teachers, and she gets to stay involved with my life.

Connecting Learning to Everything

Maya: It's not quite as good as having her here all the time, but it's not bad. It's really good to feel connected.

You may watch Denver's *Day in the Life* story as a video at http://ed-3dot0.net/cgcs/Denver.mov

---

DAY IN THE LIFE: ROCHESTER

Let these students take you on a learning journey through the newly-envisioned Rochester schools.

Narrator: It was the start of a day filled with promise and opportunity for the students in the Rochester City School District. The promise is that every student has the potential to be the best he or she can be, and the opportunity is the prospect for each student to be able to use the available technology to learn and create a place for themselves in today's and tomorrow's world.

Student 1 (on bus with device in hand): I want to know what is happening as soon as I am on my way to school. Thank God this bus is equipped with Wi-Fi, 'cause I have to check if my teacher posted the grades from my math quiz. (checks grades) Cool. I did pretty well. Hopefully, our basketball team did as well. (checks device) I got a minute before we get to school and I gotta get this drawing I did of a building in before 8 AM.

Student 2 (student at home eating breakfast and checking device as parent looks on): Hey Mom, you asked what I am doing today, here you go. (Hands device to mother or shows mom class schedule).

Mom: Looks like you're busy today. Are you going to be able to help your sister after school?

Student 2: I wish I could, but I'm manning the phones at our helpdesk for students. Not all the students are as sharp as me, mom!

Mom: I just know that last year you struggled in your Earth Science class. I don't want you waiting until the last minute.

Student 2: Don't worry about me this year. We're doing the coolest project. We're getting ready for a field trip to the river. (student checks device) Mom, I just got a text from Coach Gibson. He changed our practice until 4 o'clock tonight.

Student 3 (student checks fitness tracker as he is walking with other student who attends and stays at the campus school): Man, this fitness tracker is da bomb! But I'm finding out that I'm not as active as I should be. I need to walk at least 12,000 steps, and it's just not happening. Not only that, but I'm learning that I'm not eating the right stuff.

Student 3 friend: Where'd you get the fitness tracker? What's it for?

Student 3: The fitness tracker makes it easy to track activity, sync stats, see trends, and reach goals. We're using them in our phys ed class. It's really cool 'cause we continuously sync the stats to our computer and smartphone. We get real-time access to our progress and reminders throughout the day without having to plug anything in.

Student 3 friend: Knowing you, I think the reminders are a good idea.

Student 1 (Meets up with a couple classmates in room where academic coach is helping others) (approaches friend): I believe I know what Ms. Simmons wants for the project, but I'm not sure of the location of these buildings we're supposed to evaluate.

Student 1 friend: I say we use Google maps so we know where we're going.

Student 1: Good idea. That should save us a ton of time and work. As a matter of fact, let's put the route on our laptop instead of killing trees by printing it.

Student 2 (in science class online researching how to collect and compare water samples): Hey, I think I have the way we can collect water samples without cross-contaminating them. Hey Jamie, can you find out the best method for comparing the water samples once we get them? This is one of the coolest things we've done this year. I really didn't like science class last year. And having a laptop makes it easier and a lot more interesting than the "old school" textbooks we used last year.

Student 3 friend (learning math formulas using device to project on board) In the math class students recharge devices while working on the quadratic equation theory of black holes) (Student 3 friend sees Student 3) Hey, wanna go work out after school today?

Student 3: I can't today. I'm working the student-run helpdesk. There were a lot of students out today. Must be the flu. Anyway, during school today, the helpdesk students were busy connecting and helping the sick kids at home with whatever they needed from school. You know, with assignments and homework. We even had some of the students connect live with their class so they wouldn't miss much. The students were able to join in from home using Skype or Face Time. But let's get to-gether tonight or tomorrow.

Student 3 friend: I just remembered that I can't go to the gym either after school today. I'm going to #20 school. I'm a school-to-school mentor to some of the 4th and 5th graders.

Student 3: What's a school-to-school mentor?

Student 3 friend: It's a pretty cool deal. As part of my *Participation in Government* class, we're involved with community service projects. I chose to work with some of the little kids, and help them learn how to study and get through their work. Most of them know what to do, but there are just some kids who need real help. And to tell you the truth, I'm learning as I mentor these kids.

Student 3: That does sound cool. Did you hear what Angel is doing now? Because he's so good with Spanish, he's working at the Baden Street Center helping some of the Spanish-speaking families in the neighborhood get access to community services. And he's helping them learn how to use the computers there. He even had one woman Skype with some of her family in Puerto Rico.

Student 3 friend: Man, it looks like everybody's busy. I asked Julia if she wanted to hang out, and she's at the Eastman School working with music students over there. She's learning how to write music. The cool thing is that they all collaborate online. An Eastman student will write something, and Julia will add to it. They'll all be giving a concert later this year, so we'll see if she's as good as she says.

(Two students—Student 4 looking up the research, and Student 5 working on the course from our LMS together in a lab or library or on a bus. Student 4 flips to a digital textbook on a laptop to look up some information. Student 5 with a laptop working on an online course.)

Student 4: I'm really into my digital textbook. Ever since we started using digital textbooks, I never have to worry about losing my books, and I can use them anywhere. I really like some of the activities in the digital textbooks too. Those old school paper textbooks were deadly, weren't they?

Student 5: I totally agree. I am loving this new laptop we're using. I'm taking an RCSD (Rochester City School District) online course in computer programming. My teacher is really helpful. He is in constant contact with us. I get to keep the laptop as long as I take care of it. It's not an easy course, but I'm learning a ton, and having this laptop makes it easy to use anywhere. Instead of an hour wasted on the bus every morning, I get an hour of work done instead of just a boring ride. We're using laptops for everything now.

Student 4: Same here. I read my assignments while on the bus, and my teacher said that she likes digital textbooks because they can provide more current material than print textbooks, which can take a year or two to get to print. I like them because I don't have to carry all those books I used to carry. Now everything is in one package.

Narrator: Many of our families are below the poverty level and cannot afford costly Internet access services. But that does not preclude them from getting online. The City of Rochester has a program *Equity to Access Initiative* that grants its residents Internet access through a free "Wi-Fi blanket."

The youth of Rochester are now engaged in sustained, year-round learning as the Rochester City School District uses online instruction to extend student learning beyond the school day. Students use their district-provided devices to stay connected with their teachers, complete homework, and gain experience, knowledge, and skills through exploration. Instruction is scaffold to address the unique needs of each child. Online learning is used for initial credit classes, as well as for credit recovery and Regents review courses.

In the Rochester City School District one of our core beliefs states "we have an ethical responsibility to ensure readiness for college, career, and responsible citizenship." We believe that we can achieve our goals and help create students that are job-ready, career-ready and active citizens in the community. To help accomplish this goal we believe that we need to embrace modern technologies and teach our students how to use the technologies so that our students can achieve their fullest potential.

You may watch Rochester's *Day in the Life* story as a video at http://ed3dot0.net/cgcs/Rochester.mov

Reinvention

Reinvention begins with a vision of what the reinvented school will look like. This vision appears through the eyes of students, and follows them as they go through a day in their lives. It's developed by the students themselves, working along with their teachers, principals, curriculum folks, parents, and board members. The development and publishing of the *Day in the Life* is the first step in the reinvention process.

How to Reinvent Your School

The remainder of this chapter shows you how to lead the effort to develop a clear vision of your schools' future and create a top-level plan to get there. It provides a detailed description of a proven visioning process and helps prepare you to lead a school or district through it. Included in the appendix are several documents that may assist you in the process. First we summarize the steps in the visioning process, and then we provide instructions to help you conduct each step.

Background

You should keep in mind that it's not *your* educational vision that is being developed through this process, but the school's. The vision should reflect the needs and dreams of the many varied educational communities that comprise your school. Though no two visions will be the same, a few characteristics seem to be common to all visions developed through this process:

1. The vision is developed from the *perspective of a student,* as a description of what the student will do throughout the course of his or her learning.
2. The vision is communicated primarily through *pictures* that depict the work the student does throughout the day, accompanied by the voice of a student explaining what's happening.
3. The vision describes how digital networked technologies will be used for *teaching and learning.*

These three elements distinguish this visioning process from others, and help the school community break free of the educational jargon, checklists and abstract statements of policy that burden many other approaches to educational planning and transformation. The focus is on what the student does in the classroom, on the bus and at home as he or she learns. It forces the community to think about three key questions that school reformers and technologists seldom ask about their students:

- What's in their hands?
- What's on their minds?
- What's in their hearts?

When we pay close attention to these questions, we make a difference in students' lives. As the leader of this process, you will ask these questions many times to your participants as they reinvent their school.

Process

This multi-phase process develops a clear vision of the future of a school, and a top-level plan to get there. Working as a team, representatives of the school community examine the changing world around them, consider the energy and industry of their young people, and paint a picture of the reinvented school that serves that world and those students. Most often they imagine a school far different from the one they have today.

To see more examples of the kinds of visions produced through this process—in addition to those from Denver and Rochester described above—connect to the Education 3.0 web site at ed3dot0.net.

After creating and sharing their vision with the local community, school leaders develop a plan of action to make the changes and investments necessary to make their dreams come true: they determine the educational and technical infrastructures, policies, and practices necessary to implement their vision.

Audience

Ideally, participants in the reinvention process should *recognize the need for change,* and commit to help make it a reality. In order of importance, the key participants are students, teachers, principal(s), superintendent(s), district office leaders, parents, board members, community members, and technology experts.

The process may not be effective with the following types of groups:

1. If they are happy with the schools they have, they will not see a need for change.
2. If they are unwilling to make the changes and investments necessary to develop a forward-looking program, this process is not a good use of time and resources.
3. If there is no decision-maker in the group who can help move the action plan from vision to reality, the process will be for naught.

Participants in the process should include a broad sample of the school community. Success depends on the involvement and commitment of all, or as many as possible, of multiple points of view that each of the recommended participants brings to the table. From the beginning of the process through to the end, you need the consistent and committed involvement from all aspects of the school community—not only to create the momentum to take action, but to secure the buy-in by all constituencies, and to lead the ultimate change management. This collaborative approach builds the support needed to make the necessary transformation.

Phases

The vision and plan involves five phases, preparing for and following up on a day-long face-to-face workshop. The phases are:

- Phase 1: Preparation—1 hour
- Phase 2: Conference—3 hours
- Phase 3: Workshop—all day face-to-face meeting
- Phase 4: Production—2-3 weeks
- Phase 5: Plan—3 hours

It starts with a preparatory discussion among the school or district leadership, to discuss the purpose and outcomes of the process. Next comes a conference among a core planning group: the IT director, the instructional leader, a principal, a teacher, and a student. Here you plan the details of the face-to-face workshop day. The vision workshop day consumes six hours with everyone in the same room, where they sketch a vision of a *Day in the Life of a Student* in their reinvented school(s).

After the workshop day, the process leader or a designee develops these sketches into a slideshow with a written script. After further development by the district team—perhaps extending the slide show into a video—and circulation among key constituents, the vision presentation is used to develop a plan of what exactly needs to be done to move the school toward making its vision a reality. From beginning to end, the process at its most efficient pace takes about one month. But most schools will take at least six months, to ensure the inclusion of all points of view, and to involve the entire school community in the production of the vision.

1. Preparation

Purpose

The process leader ensures that the district is ready for and committed to the visioning process, and assembles a team of academic and technology colleagues to share leadership.

Steps

1. Identify a team of school or district leader(s) who will manage the effort and set the stage. This should include an instructional leader such as an assistant superintendent, a curriculum leader, or a principal, as well as a technical leader such as a Chief Information Officer (CIO) or Technology Coordinator.
2. Schedule a meeting of this leadership team. In preparation for this meeting, team members should review the goals and structure of the process, and look at a sample vision and plan from another school (or two or three). Several of these visions are posted online at the Education 3.0 web site at ed3dot0.net.
3. At the meeting, the team learns as much as possible about the instructional needs of the schools and the goals of the district; and discusses the vision and planning process. Here is a suggested agenda for this meeting:
   - Key colleague(s) describe the nature of the schools and the need to change.
   - The process leader explains the steps and deliverables of the visioning process.
   - All agree on dates and locations for the next two steps, the conference and the workshop.
   - All agree on additional members to serve on the core vision team (a principal, a teacher, and a student.)
4. The process leader sends a follow-up written summary of the vision and planning process, with dates and locations, to the key colleague(s).

2. Conference

Purpose

The conference of the core vision team, a three-hour meeting, allows the process leader to introduce the vision and planning process. It also sets the stage for the full-day vision workshop, and begins the process of selecting participants for it.

Participants
The participants should include these folks, or their equivalents:
- A key instructional leader;
- A principal;
- A teacher;
- A student;
- The IT director.

Pre-Work
Before the conference, the participants review online pre-work to familiarize themselves with the vision and planning process. They read, watch, or listen to podcasts of *Education 1-2-3* as well as two or three *Days in the Life*. They also review a sample *System Requirements Document* from another school, and read other relevant material on education transformation, selected by the process leader. Several of these visions are posted online at the Education 3.0 web site at ed3dot0.net.

Agenda
1. The process leader reviews the steps in the vision and planning process, and discusses the concepts set forth in the pre-work.
2. The process leader listens as the others introduce their goals and directions for reinvention. The process leader keeps the discussion focused on how the reinvention affects the work of students on the ground, in school and at home. Key questions to focus this discussion include:
   - How will the student's experience in your reinvented school differ from the way it is today?
   - As students work in your ideal school, what's in their hands? What's on their minds? What's in their hearts?
   - On the scale of Education 1-2-3, where is your school today? Where will it be after the transformation is complete? Why?
   - How does schoolwork extend beyond the school day?
   - How is the parent's role different? The teacher's?
   - How do students assess their progress in the reinvented school?

An open and frank discussion at this point is essential to the success of the vision process; it is indeed the centerpiece of this conference. The purpose of the discussion is not to arrive at any conclusion, but to get the others thinking hard about their motivation to transform. Do they indeed recognize the need for change?

3. The last segment of the conference prepares everyone for the upcoming full-day vision workshop. The discussion covers these points:

- Who's coming to the workshop? Stress the importance of involving teachers and students, as well as board members and parents. Explain that successful vision workshops have ranged from four to forty participants.
- What are the best strategies to get the workshop participants to do their pre-work before the workshop? A little preparation beforehand will make the time spent at the workshop much more productive.
- What do we need at the workshop? Review the location for the workshop and its technical capabilities. A high-quality projection system and robust internet access are essential. Tables around which teams of four or five can work, are essential. A tablet at each table, on which sketches can be drawn and then wirelessly projected to the big screen, makes for an efficient, interactive workshop.
- What will we do at the workshop? Review how the workshop will proceed (see next section) and what it will produce.
- What's my role? The process leader reviews the roles of the core vision team at the workshop.
- What's for lunch? Confirm the time, place, duration, and setting for the workshop. Take care of providing refreshments and lunch.

These should each be discussed, with the process leader or designee taking notes on the big screen as the decisions are made.

4. Follow-Up: The process leader sends an extensive follow-up written summary of this conference, with dates and locations, to the key colleague and core team.

3. Vision workshop

Purpose

The full-day, large group visioning workshop is the pinnacle of the reinvention process. At this event, the process leader and key colleagues meet face-to-face with a broad sampling of the school community. The group may include as few as half a dozen to as many as 40 participants. They should fully represent the school community: leaders, teachers, students, parents, citizens, IT staff—the more fully representative, the better.

Before the workshop, each participant completes online homework to prepare them for the day. At the workshop, they discuss their dreams for education, and then get right to work envisioning what their transformed schools will look like. Working in small groups, they sketch and script scenes from the *Day in the Life of a Student.* The workshop concludes with a presentation and discussion of the scenes.

The Vision workshop requires advanced planning to ensure quality participation by the relevant groups and to do the behind-the-scenes homework necessary to a successful day.

Invitation

At least two weeks week before the vision workshop day, the process leader sends a written invitation to workshop participants. This includes:

- Date, time location and specifics (map, security, etc.);
- Goals for the workshop;
- Reminder of and links to the pre-work that they are expected to complete;
- Contact information in case there is any problem.

A week before the workshop, the process leader sends a friend reminder, repeating this information, and asking for an RSVP.

Workshop agenda

1. **Introductions:** The first speaker at the workshop day is the highest level school leader available, such as the superintendent or board chair. In this welcome, the leader explains to participants why they are reinventing their school(s) and the importance of their contributions. The leader closes by introducing the process leader, who in turn welcomes everyone.

The leader asks each participant to introduce him or herself, and, depending on the size of the group and time available, to relate one dream for the vision.

The process leader explains how the day will proceed and what the group will produce. If students are present, the process leader makes a special point of encouraging their participation and contributions. The leader at this point also ascertains if everyone has done their homework by asking them how the historical analysis of *Education 1-2-3* applies to their local situation, and what they thought of the *Days in the Lives* that they saw.

If it seems like most participants have not done their homework, the process leader should proceed to present a shortened version of *Education 1-2-3*, and to show one of the *Days in the Lives*. Having a shared understanding of the material is crucial to the collaborative visioning process, and the participants need to start with the common references.

2. **Sketch:** This is the key element of the vision workshop, where participants draw and talk through scenes in the day in the life of a student at their reinvented school. Participants should be assembled into groups of three to six, mixed by district role. Ideally, each group includes at least one student, one teacher, one administrator, and one parent, and a board member or citizen.

The process leader reminds them of the purpose of the sketches: to illustrate an instant in the day in the life of a student through the student's eyes; and that the sketches will guide the production of the slide show. If necessary, the process leader shows a slide or two from an existing *Day in the Life* from another school, to serve as a model. The process leader also sets some guidelines for each sketch. A good sketch should:

- Illustrate what's happening from a student's perspective.
- Include specific curriculum content, with concrete examples.
- Show what's in the student's hands.
- Mention what's on the student's mind.
- Refer to what's in the student's heart.
- Show a scene that does not commonly happen today in the school.
- Illustrate a key concept in this school's transformation.

Sketch Session One: As the groups sketch in Round One, the process leader circulates to discuss what they are coming up with, and to ensure that the sketches meet the criteria listed above. For the first sketch, allow about half an hour. Encourage them to sketch right on their tablets, or with markers on a large piece of paper.

Next, each group should present and explain their sketch to the entire assembly. This is done most easily by connecting the group's tablet to the projector so that the sketches can be seen on the projection screen. Allow a few moments of discussion of each scene. Through these presentations and discussions the vision develops and solidifies in the minds of the participants. These discussions build the consensus that will produce the final vision presentation.

Sketch Session Two. After discussion, ask the groups to sketch another scene from the Day in the Life. Encourage them to choose different subjects and settings and uses of technology in this round. Allow about 20 minutes for sketching, and a half hour for presentation and discussion. Repeat the rounds until the group has generated at least a dozen scenes, representing a full day, and illustrating all aspects go the student's work.

3. **Script:** The last step in the vision workshop is for each group to write a script for each sketch. The script should simply explain what's happening from the student's perspective. The script may be written from the first person perspective ("I enter the library with my tablet in my hand ready to meet with my project group…") or the third person ("Sally enters the library with her tablet in her hand ready to meet with her project group…") The simpler, more direct script works best. Encourage the groups to avoid educational jargon, statements of belief, buzzwords or empty adjectives, and to focus on the practical and concrete. Remind them to include in their scripts answers to the following questions:

   - What's in students' hands?
   - What's on students' minds?
   - What's in students' hearts?

4. **Close of Day:** Here the process leader summarizes the events of the day: goals, processes, key points brought up in discussions, sketches, and scripts. A review of next steps—what will be done

with their work, follows. Do a quick round robin to allow all (if it is small group) or group representatives to talk about how the day went. Examples of questions might include:

- What did you learn today about possibilities for your school?
- What was your favorite part of the day?
- What would you like to do next to make your vision a reality?
- What are your next steps now that you have these ideas on paper?

Invite a key colleague to summarize and close the day. Before ending the workshop, collect the sketches and scripts, and explain how they will be produced as a slide show and returned to the leadership for review.

4. Production

Purpose
The next job for the process leader is to turn the sketches and scripts into a narrated slide show and podcast. This is best done as soon as possible after the workshop day, so that the discussions are fresh in the leader's mind.

1. **Edit the script.** Study the scripts and sketches, and determine the best order for them. They might be ordered chronologically, beginning in the morning and ending at night; or by the ages of the students, from youngest to oldest; or any other sequence that makes for a good story. Once ordered, copy and paste the scripts into a single document and edit for style. Rewrite as necessary to achieve a present-tense, practical, concrete, and consistent script that captures the spirit of the group's vision.

Notice how Denver's sketch of Tanzanians killing chickens was edited to Peruvians mining copper. The educational purpose and the technologies remained, but the content was changed to fit better with the task at hand and the sensitivities of the audience.

The process leader him or herself may not be the best person to edit the scripts. In both Denver and Rochester, folks from instruction and communications took over this task. Other districts that have gone through this visioning have involved student production or drama classes in developing the scripts into good stories.

To get ideas for style, read scripts from other visions, as posted on the Education 3.0 site at ed3dot0.net. Run the draft script past your key colleagues and selected participants in the workshop for review and comment.

2. **Draft the slides.** Copy the script scene by scene into the presenter notes section, slide by slide, in PowerPoint or Keynote. Use an existing *Day in the Life* as a model. Then add images, slide by slide, to match the script. Build in images one after the other to show action within each slide. If the school includes a teacher, staff member, or student familiar with this kind of slideshow production, encourage them to perform this work.

You may use the sketches produced at the workshop or photos provided by your schools or images drawn from the image collection posted on the Cisco Education Vision and Planning website at http://lengel. net/cisco/images/images.html.

3. **Produce slides and podcast.** Revise the slides as necessary based on feedback from your colleagues. To turn the slides into a podcast, add a voice-over narration of the script. The narrator may be the process leader, the key colleague, or (better yet) a student from the school. Also, export from the slide show a PDF file that contains the slides as well as the script. Both PowerPoint and Keynote can do this easily.

4. **Distribute.** Make the slideshow, video, or podcast available to your key colleagues, to student, faculty, and community groups, to school leaders, and to the press, in several formats:

   - The text of the script;
   - A slideshow in PowerPoint or Keynote;
   - A PDF file of the slideshow with notes;
   - A narrated podcast;
   - A video.

5. **Promote.** Circulate the Day in the Life among the participants in the workshop day and to the school community. This is best done by posting the variously-formatted files online where they can easily be viewed and downloaded by all, perhaps on the school or district's web site.

5. Plan

Purpose
To turn the vision illustrated by your Day in the Life into a plan of action, you will create two new documents:

Behind the scenes. This version of the slideshow or video adds callouts that show the technical and educational infrastructures necessary behind the scenes, to make each scene possible. Both PowerPoint and Keynote include text boxes and speech bubbles to make this an easy process. You can see an example of such a document on the Cisco Education Vision and Planning web site at http://lengel.net/cisco/vision/DITL_Texas_BTS.pdf.

System requirements. The spreadsheet in Figure 9-1 takes each element of each scene, and spells out the technical, educational, and policy changes that need to occur in the school or district to make these scenes a reality. A sample System Requirements document is attached as an appendix to this chapter (see Figure 9-2). Instructions for preparing this spreadsheet are also included in the appendix.

.

Item	July	August	September	October	November	December	January	Feb
Technical Infrastructure								
Each student carries a digital device suitable for their SEN/AI work.	Write specs for digital device.	Get bids for devices.	Purchase devices.	Provide devices to teachers.	Provide devices to students.	Monitor use of devices.	Monitor use of devices.	Monitor us devices.
The school provides a robust wireless network enables all devices to connect securely, with bandwidth and protocols for rich media products, bandwidth and protocols for web conferencing, standards-based protocols to permit advanced and multi-user applications.	Write specs for network capacity. Conduct network analysis and tests.	Get bids for network improvements.	Install improved network. Test network.	New network in operation.	Monitor network operation.	Monitor network operation.	Monitor network operation.	Monitor ne operation.
The school provides network services and software to monitor various networked laboratory instruments, and to enable a secure, private, campus-wide multimedia messaging system.	Write specs for network software.	Get bids for network software.	Install network software. Test operation.	Network software in operation.	Monitor network software.	Monitor network software.	Monitor network software.	Monitor ne software
The school provides a system to store and manage digital media products built by students and by teachers, usable by industry experts to access selected student work products, in an online digital library connecting a variety of digital media sources, providing access to online learning materials any time, any place, any time.		Write specs for digital media storage system.	Get bids for digital media storage system.	Install media storage system.	Populate media storage system with academic content.	Populate media storage system with academic content.	Populate media storage system with academic content.	Populate m storage sy academic
The school provides a learning management system that can index all learning materials, and manage digital media, teach competencies and track student progress, store, manage, and track progress through online tutorials, administer, record, and track various forms of assessment of student progress, record and track group progress through project assignments, and download learning materials to any device.	Write specs for LMS.	Get bids for LMS.	Install LMS.	Populate LMS with course content.	Populate LMS with course content.	Populate LMS with course content.	Populate LMS with course content.	Use LMS and learni
The school provides web conferencing systems that are standards-based, for communication with local industries; with video, audio, text, and screen-sharing; that can work from desktops, laptops, or tablets.			Write specs for web conferencing systems.	Get bids for web conferencing systems.	Install web conferencing systems.	Monitor use of web conferencing systems.	Monitor use of web conferencing systems.	Monitor us conferenci systems.
Networked digital sensors are available in all laboratories, where lab instruments connected as appropriate to network and devices.		Write specs for lab sensors.	Get bids for lab sensors.	Install and test lab sensors.	Use lab sensors in teaching and learning.	Use lab sensors in teaching and learning.	Use lab sensors in teaching and learning.	Use lab se teaching a learning.
Curriculum Development								
Learning materials are all available in digital form.	Set standards for digital learning materials.	Develop digital learning materials.	Develop digital learning materials.	Develop digital learning materials.	Post digital learning materials to LMS.	Post digital learning materials to LMS.	Post digital learning materials to LMS.	Use digital in teaching learning.
Interdisciplinary project assignments developed and posted, that focus on real-world social and technical issues worth solving, include local industry connections, embed industry competencies, include online research and milestones for tracking student progress.	Set standards for interdisciplinary projects.	Develop interdisciplinary projects.	Develop interdisciplinary projects.	Develop interdisciplinary projects.	Post interdisciplinary projects to LMS.	Post interdisciplinary projects to LMS.	Post interdisciplinary projects to LMS.	Use interd projects in and learnin
Advanced technical courses are designed and posted.	Set specs for advanced technical	Develop advanced technical courses.	Develop advanced technical courses.	Develop advanced technical courses.	Develop advanced technical courses.	Develop advanced technical courses.	Post advanced courses to LMS.	Post advan courses to

Figure 9-1

APPENDIX

Sample Instructions and Homework for Workshop Participants from the Process Leader

Hello <Participant Name>,

Welcome to the XYZ Schools' Vision Workshop.

With this message I explain the workshop, and assign your homework to be completed by <the workshop date>. Please pass this along to anyone else that you know will be attending the workshop. Feel free to contact me with any questions or suggestions. I'll see you on <the workshop date>.

(Don't worry, the homework is all online, and will take about 45 minutes to compete.)

<Process Leader's Name>, <email >, <phone>, <instant message address>

What is the Vision Workshop?

The Vision Workshop is designed to help us develop a clear vision of the future of XYZ schools, and begin development of a high-level plan to get there. Working as a team, our school community will examine the changing world around us, consider the energy and industry of our young people, and paint a picture of the schools we need to serve that world and those students. I expect we will imagine schools quite different from the ones we have. We'll be reinventing school.

After sharing this vision with the community, we'll develop a plan to make the changes and investments necessary to make our dream come true—the educational and technical infrastructures, policies, funding, and practices necessary to each element of our vision.

Before participating in the workshop, it is important that you recognize the need for change—if you are happy with the schools we have or are not willing to make the changes and investments necessary to develop a better program, then you are not a good candidate for the workshop.

The workshop will proceed in five phases, centering on the day-long face-to-face workshop scheduled for <date and day>:

1. Preparation: XYZ schools leadership, both instructional and technical, worked together in <month> to plan the visioning process.

2. Conference: A select group of XYZ school leaders worked with me to plan the details of the <workshop date> workshop day.

3. Workshop: The big workshop day on <workshop date> involves six hours, where you and a cross section of the XYZ school community will sketch a vision of a *Day in the Life of a Student* in our transformed schools.

4. Production: After the workshop day, my team will develop your sketches into a slideshow with a written script. After further development by our leadership team, and circulation among key constituents, the slideshow will be used to develop a plan of what exactly needs to be done to move XYZ schools toward its vision.

5. Plan: Given your vision, we will develop a plan to execute the vision over the short and long term: the educational and technical infrastructures, policies, funding, and practices necessary to each element of our vision.

Many schools have worked their way through this process, and you will be reviewing their results along the way to help you understand the elements you might include in your vision and plan.

What Will We Do on <Workshop Date>?

We will work through a process of envisioning transformed schools. We'll begin with a discussion of our dreams of a student fully engaged with technology and learning. We'll brainstorm a *Day in the Life of a Student* in XYZ as it will be transformed. We'll develop the brainstorm into a series of sketches, share them, and detail them with scripts.

What's the Result?

At the end of the day on <workshop date>, we will have a rough draft of a *Day in the Life* of a student in XYZ. My team will work these up into a slide show or video, which we will discuss with our school community. Once we've discussed it in this way, we will turn the *Day in the Life* into a Plan of Action for what we need to do next to lead our schools to their new vision.

What's My Role?

Your role is to participate fully in the process of visioning and planning: to complete your homework before the <...day's> session, and to encourage other members of the team to contribute fully to the discussions as they sketch their Day in the Life.

What's My Homework?

Before our conference on <workshop date>, you'll do these assignments:

1. Read or watch *Education 1-2-3*.
2. Read or watch the *Days in the Life* of at least two schools.
4. Dream about what a *Day in the Life* would look like for your transformed school.

All of these (except #4) can be found online at ed3dot0.net

Instructions for Developing System Requirements

How to Extract Your System Requirements from Your Vision of a Day in the Life of a Student

The student in your vision presentation carries out a multitude of educational tasks during the day. Each of these tasks calls for some sort of technology, sometimes traditional (a book, for instance), sometimes digital (a computer). The sum of all the technologies required by students and teachers to carry out their respective tasks is called your *system requirements*. These are the technologies and related items you'll need to accomplish your vision.

You don't need an engineer to design your system requirements. You can do it yourself by studying closely your vision presentation, and following through on what you see there. You'll do this on a spreadsheet, as shown below. Here's how.

1. Describe a learning activity. Look at the first slide or scene of your vision presentation. What is your student doing? What kind of learning activity is he engaged in? Let's say that in the first slide he is connecting to his online biology course from home just before breakfast, to download some illustrated readings to his tablet for study on his way to school. That's the learning activity. You'll put this in the first column of the System Requirements Template. To make the template easier to understand, you'll describe the learning activity a bit more generically: students download to mobile devices multimedia assignments and resources from home and school. This learning activity will dictate the kinds of technologies you will need.

2. Describe the hardware in the student's hands. Start with what's in her hands, the hardware on which she'll download the assignment. In this case it's a tablet, a common mobile learning device. So, in the second column of the template, labeled Hardware, you'll enter *mobile device with internet connectivity and multimedia capabilities.* It's important here to spell out exactly what the hardware needs to do, in this case be small enough to be carried and used on the bus or subway (tablet-sized), able to connect to the server where the assignment is stored (internet connectivity), able to display the illustrated reading from the online biology course (multimedia capabilities.) If your description is not complete, you may not get what you need.

3. Describe the software the student needs on that hardware. Don't assume the device will come out of the box with the software the student needs, and don't assume that the standard programs will suffice. Be specific in what you enter on the template in the third column, Local Software. This student will need an internet browser to connect to the Learning Management System (LMS) that holds the biology course, as well as a program to save and display the text and the images in the lesson. So enter Web browser with multimedia display and storage capability. List only the software the device needs for the student to accomplish the learning activity in the first column.

4. Describe the network services required for this learning activity. If the student could accomplish this task without connecting to the network, then you'd leave this column blank. But in the case at hand, the student needs a solid network connection from his device at home to the school's LMS. And since most mobile devices use wireless connections, include this fact in your description: Wireless web-based access to LMS system from home and school. Restrict this column to connectivity services; server software (such as the LMS) will go in column six.

5. Describe the network infrastructure needed for this learning activity. Here is where you describe the servers and routers and other hidden items that are so essential to enabling this learning activity. You may need some help from a technology consultant to complete this description (or you may copy from one of the examples in the System Requirements Sample). Your description might be: Server capacity for multiple online course storage, along with bandwidth and port access sufficient for multimedia downloading.

6. Describe the server software necessary to this learning activity. The kind of online biology course you envision in this learning activity calls for an LMS, stocked with multimedia biology content suitable for the ninth grade, and aimed at the Regent's exam and formatted for mobile devices. Again, the description must be specific; not just any biology course will suffice to put into your student's hands the materials she needs, when and how she needs them. Write your system requirements to force the lowest bidder to provide you exactly what you need. The System Requirements Sample can provide you with some useful wording.

7. Describe the skills teachers will need to make this learning activity happen. The downloading at home and study on the subway will never occur unless the teacher works this assignment into the biology course. Most teachers have never taught with the assistance of an online course or a mobile device, so teacher development becomes a system requirement. Describe it here in the second-to-last column: How to integrate a Learning Management System and mobile devices into the everyday curriculum.

8. Describe the skills students will need to make this learning activity happen. We sometimes assume that our students already possess the technology skills they need to do the kind of learning activity we envision. Don't be so sure. List student development as a system requirement for each activity. In the current instance it might be: How to access assignments from LMS, download them to a mobile device, and learn with them outside of school.

What you have just done is to take a single scene from your vision, and work it back through the network of devices, software, services and

Learning Activity	Hardware	Local Software	Network Services	Network Infrastructure	Server Software	Teacher Development	Student Development	Policy	Responsible	Budget
Parents use online workstation	Personal computer with full multimedia capabilities	Web browser, video capability	Management of school information (curriculum, school store, lunch, etc.)	Robust network with high bandwidth to digital media display.	Storage, management, and distribution of curriculum and other school information (database)	Use learning management database to store and track curriculum.	Learn, and then teach parents to use curriculum and other school information (database)			
Superintendent appears by videoconference	Digital media display	Videoconference software	Videoconference delivery and origination to digital display.	Robust network with high bandwidth to handle videoconferencing.	Videoconference management					
Video of partner school in South Africa	Digital media display		Video storage and delivery to digital display.	Robust network with high bandwidth to digital media display.	Video storage and management and distribution.	Global collaborative project design. Video production and digital editing.	Global collaborative project work. Video production and digital editing.			
Solar energy curriculum project	Computers or tablets with science probe capabilities	Probeware, data analysis, data display, drawing, science content	Wireless and wired connections to science instruments	Robust, standards-based network to science data	Science content management	Use of project-based learning and science probes	Project-based learning and science probes.			

Figure 9-2. Sample of a System Requirements document

skills that are necessary to make it happen. If your vision presentation shows what's on stage, the system requirements show what's behind the scenes. And as you can see, there's quite a bit of work to be done back there.

So, continue on: take each and every scene in your *Day in the Life,* describe it as a learning activity, and walk it back through to the various system requirements. Not all learning activities will show an entry into each column, but most will involve several behind the scenes requirements. Don't be afraid to use the System Requirements Template for ideas—we compiled this from the work of more than a dozen schools just like yours.

Don't worry about repetition—you'll find that the same system requirement shows up over and over again (such as *robust standards-based network available from school and home)* as being required for many different learning activities. The more times a requirement shows up in the template, the more important it is to your vision. Feel free to copy and paste as you complete the template.

Once your System Requirements Template is complete, take it to your information technology staff, or to your technology vendors, and ask them to design the system for you, columns two through six. Take it also to your professional development staff and to your curriculum people, and ask them to look at the first and the last two columns and plan accordingly to deliver the goods.

JIM LENGEL *is the author of* Education 3.0, Education 1.2.1, *and eight other books on education, communication, and technology. His teaching career began in 1971 as a Peace Corps volunteer, and includes 46 years of work at the elementary, secondary, and university levels. He earned degrees at Yale College and the Harvard Graduate School of Education, served as the Deputy Commissioner of Education for the State of Vermont, and as consultant to Apple, Cisco, IBM, Sony, Microsoft, Amplify, and dozens of schools and colleges around the world. His work focuses on the application of new technologies to teaching and learning, and the improvement of teaching through video analysis. He can be reached at jim@lengel.net.*

10

Governance that Works

Leslie Wilson

Education leaders cannot stand on the sidelines allowing obstacles to divert attention from educators doing the right work with learners. This chapter is a *call to action* for those who govern local, district, state, and national education organizations. The time is now to understand and retool expertise to effectively lead schools today and into the future. Education governance matters deeply for effective education and digital transformation. It is a major lever in advancing digitally transformed learning. Learning-focused educational technology programs are launched from a vibrant vision of desired outcomes, and a firm grasp of how robust mobile devices and information and communication technologies (ICT) can help schools achieve them.

Changes to the central education systems will not happen without vital leadership and supporting culture. This must be a guided evolution as the school and district mature within a continuous cycle of improvement. It cannot be an episodic anecdote. The system's values and norms are inspired by its leadership and the stakeholders who work for and affect its operation.

This IS leadership for second-order change. It is not about "tinkering" around the edges of 19th and 20th century education model. It is fundamentally a systemic shift that requires most stakeholders having to retool and jump on a continuous learning curve. Leading in these environments requires deep knowledge of curriculum, instruction, and meaningful integration of technologies. It further demands the leaders understand the human condition when embarking on any diversion from "the way we do things around here." Individuals and groups will require support and guidance in how not only to travel the transformational path, but also how it will affect their craft, practice, roles, and relationships.

Change naturally accompanies implementation of any school reform, targeted student outcomes, and integration of technologies. Authentic "change" is systemic. It is considering all the systems at work in a district and school, and determining how they will sync together once it is determined what will change and what will stay the same. Policies, processes, services, communications, knowledge, and technologies are part of the bigger picture. A school culture that expects stakeholders to create a learning environment where colleagues collaborate using data effectively, will help shift practice and expectations for educators to imagine things as they could be, not as they are.

> Authentic "change" is systemic. It is considering all the systems at work in a district and school, and determining how they will sync together once it is determined what will change and what will stay the same.

Technologies have taken root in America's classrooms. Some schools and districts clear the path with policies, system redesign, and professional growth models to advance digital conversions. This lays groundwork for successful, meaningful technology integrations and scale.

Other scenarios are marked by technology purchases and deployments using the leadership's "spray and pray" model. Devices are distributed without vision and planning in the *hope* that desired educational outcomes will somehow emerge. Then there are the instances where leaders' good intentions, policy, and plans accompany the digital transformation, but competing priorities and mandates stymie and confuse innovation and progress.

In the latter landscape, educators are pressured to double down on preparing students for standardized tests, and other state/federal mandates to the exclusion of being able to organically grow self and learner competencies that lead to ubiquitous use of education technology tools. Mandates, standards. and other external pressures are realities. Strategies to minimize their impact are essential.

Leaders must steer the course to avoid obstructions caused by overdosed attention to high stakes tests outcomes, teachers' performance assessment tied to same, and the negative culture that accompanies those situations. A starting point can be garnering the shared stakeholders' understanding of what learners *need* to flourish, achieve full potential and be next-generation inventors and innovators.

Effective leaders drive tactical paces that enable educators' moral imperative to include: how student-centric learning models will be the foundation of their work; how educational technologies can galvanize learners and teachers for productivity and success; knowing the prospective impact and objectives of transformative educational technology implementations. However, often overlooked is the support of a school's primary work which is teaching. This requires the testing of teachers yet at the same time overcoming the tendency of discouraging risk-taking and creativity. Educators must establish environments of exploration, higher order problem-solving, and thought processing and personalized paths for each learner.

Getting There

It may sound redundant and trite to say that a district's governance and building level leaders must nurture a common vision driving strategy and practice. Superior leaders know this, and make certain that the process for defining, amplifying, and implementing the vision becomes everyone's reality. The vision and mission, as led by key and distributed leaders, is to prepare youth for a globally-linked world both to ensure their successful citizenry and that of local, state, and national communities.

The education system exists to serve learners, local, state, and broader communities. With a focus on students, fundamental beliefs and practices must serve their development of full potential. In this day and age it further calls upon the moral imperative of ensuring learners' consistent, meaningful, and uninterrupted access to technology tools of the day.

A reaffirmation of the primary purpose for the district's and school's existence is of utmost importance. It's also important to be clear on that which is NOT the reason for being. Environments where teachers and learners are blasted with fear and fury to "achieve" on high stakes tests, and adhere to other external mandates "or else" diminish joy, progress, and efficacy for all stakeholders. Results are not achieved overnight. Results are not achieved through fear of punishment, or reprisal, or hammering students with regurgitation, memorization. and teaching to the almighty test.

High quality leadership must get to the core purpose of the work in order to lay the groundwork for systemic overhaul of "managing by coercion and threat." Questions such as these that follow will drive a shared definition of courses of action, strategies, values. and principles.

- What is our purpose?
- What is our vision with learners at the core?
- What beliefs and values drive our interactions?
- How do we keep learners as the nucleus of quality decision-making regarding practice and systems?
- What is the description of a successful graduate?

To answer the last question brings to bear the thoughtful consideration of competing priorities. Yes, the community and parents/caregivers expect high academic achievement tied to standards. Yes, they want learners prepared for post-high school education and careers. Yes, there is consensus that we want our young people to emerge as global citizens with working knowledge and skills in how to navigate and succeed in an information rich age supported by a myriad of current and emerging tech tools.

There are ways to pull open the door to address competing mandates while growing and moving to an effective digital conversion. A systemic approach is the only way forward to be certain learners and educators can fully advance the digital system. Staffing, budgeting, teacher evaluation, assessments, grading, promotion, quality control measures are all part of the needed systemic shift. The district and school leadership teams must be aligned in realizing that the traditional focus on mandates and pressures isn't best serving learners in a holistic approach.

A shift in a governance model compels personal dedications from district and school leaders to foster collaborative leadership and management techniques. Broad study, stakeholder feedback, personal reflection, collaborative dialogue, and coaching

> A shift in a governance model compels personal dedications from district and school leaders to foster collaborative leadership and management techniques.

with peers are necessary to make personal leadership changes. The pathway to shifting leadership strategies will be unique to each individual although the focus across the board must

Highly effective leaders govern in ways that elicit respect.

be on creating and sustaining learning organizations that successfully lead to a digital transformation that advances student achievement.

Highly effective leaders govern in ways that elicit respect. Expertise and experience are important. They have ownership of their actions and are responsible to constituents. While they don't always have immediate solutions, they give guidance and inspiration to collaborate with others toward common goals. In essence, they are about continuous learning in partnership with all stakeholders.

A key ingredient for any transformation, initiative, new program, or shift in culture is the redundancy of high quality leaders who possess the same beliefs, sense of mission and vision that are fundamental to the movement. This distributed leadership model will ensure forward progress, evaluation and adjustment of the new practices in place now and into the future. More about this will be discussed in a later segment of this chapter.

Top leaders in a digital transformation require qualities in tandem with vision to make clear the journey of practice for teachers, learners and greater community. In addition to creating the landscape in which the whole child and not only mandate/dictate response practice exists, governance for this generation must:

- Possess and clearly articulate a strong belief system aligned with shared vision and mission.
  - This amplifies resolve to moderate if not eliminate the external mandates that fly in the face of effective technology integration.
- Have a deep knowledge base about what is entailed for a high quality digital transformation.
- Muster the understanding that the digital transformation is not happening for its own sake, but for the purpose of providing learners an ecosystem that mirrors tool usage prevalent across the globe.
- Align the digital adoption with evidence-based decision-making.

- Regularly share the evidence-based decision-making, research and best practices with that are the foundation for the digital movement.
- Share in the responsibility for results.
- Challenge outdated customs and practices that don't align with the vision.
- Create an ecosystem that identifies *all areas* of success measures beyond state/federal mandates and dictates.
- Establish and maintain a state of art communications and feedback plan among all stakeholders.
  - This includes efficiencies in troubleshooting and problem-solving procedures.
- Know group's and individual's thresholds of joy and exasperation to inform pace and practice
- Be decisive, honest, and direct.

The common mission and vision embolden the extended team to execute strategies together for the sake of whole child development.

Core Work: Serve the Whole Child

Savvy educators understand the requisite of "the whole child approach." This compels a move from a limited definition of academic achievement to one that entails a wide-ranging, long-term plan for growth and success of each child. This takes, invariably, the embracing community for it to be collaborative and sustainable. The foundation of education focuses on every child being safe, healthy, engaged, supported, and challenged to reach his/her full potential. The focus is to be on comprehensive learner-centric development with high stakes tests, drastic accountability measures, and other mandates taking a backseat or a sidecar to what is in the learners' best interest.

Defining the latter gives a compass for navigating the swirling winds of expectations and what is defined as "progress." Given time, resources, tools, and professional learning

> Given time, resources, tools, and professional learning needed to succeed, teachers can muster the breathing room to see and plan beyond narrow definitions of learner success and pursue a more learner-centered approach.

needed to succeed, teachers can muster the breathing room to see and plan beyond narrow definitions of learner success and pursue a more learner-centered approach.

Educational technology initiatives are about enabling students to achieve their greatest potential. Leaders make certain that all the elements of the system line up to make that happen. This requires changes throughout the system—improving curriculum resources and professional learning, teacher evaluation systems tied to growth and coaching, finding sustainable funding, creating policies that support it, and then creating a continuous cycle of innovation and improvement.

This is hard, courageous work. It takes time and patience. There's not room for the leaders' egos to drive competition derived by test scores. Obstacles can be digested in ways that give energy to meaningful digital reform. We change the environment and work through the challenges by keeping the focus on serving every learner in the best possible ways.

Boots on the Ground

Authentic, comprehensive learning environments, in lieu of a garish, hard-driven teach to the test and accountability model, are non-negotiable *when creating learner-centric ecosystems.* Leadership matters tremendously, both to bring stakeholders together and to manage this deep, systemic approach. All perspectives must be counted and part of this process. Forward movement must continue.

For those who don't believe, show them the research and data. There are comprehensive transformation models, research to back it up, and expert practitioners who can help. Effective leadership teamed with a systematic approach can make it happen. In this scenario, stakeholders share a common vision, and work together to make changes happen throughout the system. It's the "team" that is banded together bottom-up around the strategic vision that are foundational. Some questions to drive the work: Are we producing deep thinkers, problem-solvers, innovators, scientists, and engineers at the rate we need? Are children becoming less creative as they age in school? Are we enhancing or diminishing the growth mindsets of teachers and learners? Are students dropping out at higher rates? Are they motivated? Examine the data, and figure out what it's telling us we need to do.

A full-on working distributed leadership team with common purpose lays the groundwork for overcoming the roadblocks. First, affirmation of purpose and strategies that lead to the realization of that purpose are ground rules. Second, any factors that force diversion from said purpose must be acknowledged and addressed so they either become peripheral, fully integrated, or take a back seat to what is most important.

Courage, persistence, and communication are hallmarks of transformative leaders who clear the path for educators and learners to do the right work. How can these leaders protect and pursue the sanctity of principled work in light of dictates, mandates and pressures?

- Communicate the school's/district's affirmation of priorities to all stakeholders. While increased student achievement is a top goal, the methods for reaching this outcome will be meaningful and personalized for each learner within a broader culture of care and understanding. Local, state, and federal levels need to be informed.
- Define short- and long-term roadmaps for reaching achievement goals.
- Share access to the district's guaranteed content and curriculum highlighting alignment with state and federal standards.
- Connect the above with the goals relative to the dictates and mandates. Demonstrate how the school's/district's priorities are complimentary not contradictory.
- Communicate anticipated timeline and project plan for achieving the outlined priorities with regular reporting guidelines.
- Create frequent checkpoints to measure progress. Be transparent in sharing results.
- Provide rationale and research that demonstrates the efficacy of individual's learning that is tailored to his/her unique qualities and needs. This tied to a meaningful technology integration can double the rate of learning.
- Be courageous in challenging the dictates and threats imposed by unrealistic expectations of student achievement within unrealistic timelines.
- Know that there may be consequences, and be prepared to accept and adjust to them.

■ Ensure strong connections with internal and external stakeholder groups and communities so they understand and support the school's/district's direction and related courses of action. They need to know the school's/district's priorities, strategies, and commitment to the same goals should be imposed by mandates/dictates even though their path may be different from others'.

Of course the above exercises and practices need to be affirmed and adopted by school board members, and central office, and building administrators. Board members and superintendent will require courage to stand tall in supporting their priorities to local, state and federal leaders. There may be risk attached. Those can be proactively addressed.

In districts labeled "failing" the bar is often set high above reach. Administrators commonly have responded with "hair on fire" strategies that not only frighten teachers and students but also the extended community. There is a need for honest "town hall" meetings aimed at explaining the current state of affairs, while often not pretty, presenting strategies for addressing them go a long way. Realistic expectations play a major role. If the school is failing, compared to state/national averages, across the board, it will be daunting if not improbable that those ratings will be dramatically increased in a year. So, what are realistic expectations? What will the school/district be doing to get there? What can parents/caregivers do to support these common goals? What intermediate assessments/measures will be shared with all stakeholders to gauge progress?

The above tactics address external factors. Internally, the following strategies will help guide the ability to work with and around the obstacles so they become part of the ecosystem—not its main artery. The real lifeblood, the "real" work lies in the personalized learning approach within a technology powered-up structure. The process is not linear or rigid. It is fluid and adjustable. These strategies, when executed with all stakeholders, will drive focus of practice and expectations.

■ Define tenets of day-to-day priorities—school and classroom.

■ Define school-/district-wide student achievement and other goals with measures besides high stakes tests that will drive those outcomes.

■ Ensure district's guaranteed curriculum is aligned with state, federal standards.

- Identify teaching and learning design that builds student voice and agency.
  - Provide consistent, ongoing professional learning for the above.
- Ensure that administrators and teachers can collaborate in a teacher evaluation model that encourages professional growth, openness to risk-taking, peer-to-peer coaching, and open door feedback.
- Pinpoint the operations that impede any of the above noted priorities.
- Identify new procedures to ameliorate those impediments.
- Enhance formative assessments around transparent learning goals for each student.
- Teachers and learners perform the above exercises in each class or grouping creating partnership and culture of learning *not focused on high stakes test performance.*
- Create a cycle of continuous improvement keeping everyone focused on goals.
- Report progress to internal and stakeholders and make adjustments as needed.
- Provide teachers with collaborative planning tools that help students direct their learning and what they need to achieve at higher rates.
- Allow teachers and learners to organize intentional time for students to reflect on their progress, giving opportunity for learners to consider what and how they learned.

Backward design or backward mapping[1] is a strategy to design learning activities and instruction aimed at learning goals. It is a way for teachers and students to create content, curriculum, assessments, and demonstrations of learning. The process if well integrated with the digital conversion goals can be expeditious, just in time, and provide immediate feedback. With this structure in place, teachers, leaders, and learners can continue to focus in a personalized manner on progress, needs, interventions, and remediation. This is an ideal way to blend the priorities of standards based teaching while meaningfully integrating technologies.

---

[1] http://edglossary.org/backward-design/

Back mapping[2] would be a good tool for the above deliberations. The process is driven with the end in mind defined. It is a results-oriented practice where teachers analyze student data, assess his/her knowledge and abilities, seek and engage professional growth opportunities, and embrace a coaching/mentoring model with peers and school leaders.

Governance Capacity and Sustainability

Reality is that leaders leave. They move on to next opportunities, retire, and the like. The vast majority of programs and transformations that fail are due to a lack of leadership and will to carry on the important work when a key leader leaves. In complex transformations such as this discussion around digital conversions, the organization must be nimble, flexible, and yet structured. This calls on a multi-team and distributed leadership structure for support, assessments, communications, and adjustments.

There will likely always be a point leader in place-a person for whom, as they say, "the buck stops here." Key, quick decisions and actions may be required through the course of the movement. The top person can be charged with execution of those times. These are usually best gotten after by a single person with that authority granted rather than delaying needed action by trying to call together meetings to make decisions.

District/school leadership is really about stewardship and mentoring. Top leaders recognize others' strengths, and help unlock their capacities and potential broadening the band of leader achievers. This is a way to create more leaders for the conversion, ensuring there is an expanded pool of those who can be as effective, if not more so, than those in top leadership roles.

Early on in program movement, these leaders with top leadership,

> District/school leadership is really about stewardship and mentoring. Top leaders recognize others' strengths, and help unlock their capacities and potential broadening the band of leader achievers.

---

[2] https://www2.ed.gov/admins/tchrqual/learn/nclbsummit/gentile/edlite-slide005.html

should be identified, should participate in common professional learning about leading change, and create a learning community that is based on serving constituents toward reaching goals. These leaders must be visible, available, and knowledgeable. Within their community of practice they can, together, reflect on practices, challenges, and solutions.

In the bigger picture, conflicts will emerge. Stressors will abound. Many moving parts will require attention and guidance. The team/program leaders can share in this work across the board. Having the common mission binding their work, their ability to handle situations that arise will be consistent in word and practice toward reaching the overarching goals.

Communications play a major role in this redundancy of leadership activity. An important message overlooked or downplayed can cause a ripple effect of harm to forward progress and practice. Teachers need to know that productively engaging with the transformation will not have negative repercussions on their evaluations or professional courage. Consistent messaging across distributed leaders will ensure a bond focused on purpose. It will also keep open a 360-degree operation to respond and proactively address emerging issues. There is safety among educators when they realize they will not be penalized for taking risks, making mistakes, or failing in the line of action.

> "Pervasive leadership has a greater likelihood of occurring if leaders work on mastering the five core capacities: moral purpose, understanding of the change process, building relationships, knowledge building, and coherence making."
> —MICHAEL FULLAN

Conclusion

This is a call to action for education leaders across all spectrums. Utilizing the strategies outlined in this chapter will facilitate learner-centric digital transformations in the face of bureaucracy, regulations, mandates, and unrealistic expectations. In his book *Leading in a Culture of Change* (2007) Michael Fullan said: "Pervasive leadership has a greater likelihood of occurring if leaders work on mastering the five core capacities: moral purpose, understanding of the change process, building relationships, knowledge building, and coherence making." The above narrative outlines those key capacities and practices required for a successful digital transformation.

Today's leaders need to move obstacles so that educators' moral imperative and focused purpose are at the core of their work. This kind of leading is challenging. It requires courage, honesty, and sometimes reversing the course of reckless mandates and unrealistic expectations to best serve learners' achievement.

The distributed leadership team is essential to this effort. Titles and roles aren't perquisites. Skills, knowledge of craft, research, culture, and understanding the human response to change are necessary ingredients.

LESLIE WILSON *is the CEO and co-founder of One-to-One Institute, a non-profit organization serving in successful implementation of personalized 1:1 learning programs. She earlier co-directed Michigan's 1:1 initiative, Freedom to Learn.*

Prior to working in the Institute, Ms. Wilson served public education for 31 years as a change agent, teacher, and multiple administrator roles. An Education Policy/Program Fellow with the Institute for Educational Leadership, Ms. Wilson created an advanced fellowship program for educational technology leaders. She completed her undergraduate and doctoral coursework at the University of Michigan, has a Master of Arts in Instructional Technology from Wayne State University, and special education administrator certification from Eastern Michigan University. She is currently Board President of Nexus Academy, Lansing, Michigan, a blended learning high school and a mentor for Intel's Education Accelerator Project.

11

IT² When Information Technology and Instructional Technology Communicate and Collaborate Great Things Can Happen: Vision for the District as a Whole

Dr. Mel Pace

In theory, the Vision for a school district is set by the Superintendent. That may be actually true for the general vision but it is not, in my experience, true when it comes to a vision for technology in a school district. I have worked in four different school districts; all, by national standards, large to very large districts. I have known some very visionary leaders who, when they became the Superintendent, just simply lost that capacity. I think it has to do with the daily stress of the politics of running a school district, no matter the size.

One of the most frustrating times of my life occurred when a district's test scores had fallen, and the Superintendent announced that he was going to put together a committee to study the issue. I immediately asked the Assistant Superintendent who was to chair this committee to be allowed to be a member. I was informed that the committee had already been formed and met, and that they had determined that there was nothing new that could be done to change those scores. Wow! Talk about being floored. I was so dumb founded that I just walked out of their office. Wow! Nothing new. Really ?????

Equally frustrating is watching a leader with a great vision who lacks the personal communication skills to communicate that vision and gain support for it. We had a new Superintendent come into our district from a very large district. He was dynamic and laser focused on student achievement. However, someone had told him the he "needed to show these people how it is done." Well, he proceeded to do so, and within two years was literally run out of the district. What he wanted to do was amazing and desperately needed in our district, but he just tried cramming all of the changes down peoples' throats without even getting to know the culture of the district before beginning to make those changes.

So, having a vision is great, but if you cannot communicate it there is no value in spending the time to develop that vision. Likewise, seeing a vision that includes little consideration for the learning styles of 21st century learners is heartbreaking, especially for those in the Instructional Technology field who watch students being forced into 20th century learning patterns that are foreign to them. Nothing new? Wow! We have nothing but new ways of engaging these students.

Vision for Instructional Technology

I entered my most recent position as Director of Media and Instructional Technology in 2007. Upon coming to my new district I found that we were opening three new schools. To my horror, we were also placing analog televisions in every classroom. Although two of the three schools were all but complete, and the televisions were already ordered and brackets were already in place for them, I was able to pull together the money to begin placing LCD projectors in those schools. We later were able to come back, and get interactive whiteboards in most of the new classrooms. By the time the third school was ready for occupancy in midyear we had also been able to upgrade most of the technology in that school.

Our first true "21st Century" school opened in August 2008 with the full range of LCD projectors, document cameras, interactive whiteboards, and audio amplification in every classroom. When asked how I could afford to add all of this new technology I simply said, "By taking out all of the stuff that is no longer useful." The things that we removed were: all of the coaxial cable, a very expensive media distribution system, the old overhead projectors, and televisions. With the money that we saved, we installed a new digital delivery system and enhanced the digital content by purchasing additional streaming content.

Over the next seven years we would build four new schools, completing total rebuilds of two high schools and one elementary school, adding five new wings, and finishing a number of renovation projects. In each case the new technology package was a part of the construction plan. In addition, many schools were able to secure funding through various sources to bring other classrooms up to the new standard.

As should be the case, the Vision changed over those seven years. By the time I retired in October of 2015 we had several schools with strong Bring Your Own Device (BYOD) programs and 1:1 initiatives, and newer forms of interactivity were being explored for our classrooms. It became apparent that although interactive whiteboards had brought some additional interactivity and engagement to our classrooms, today's students needed that interactivity in their own hands. Exploration of a variety of interactive modes in the classrooms is currently underway. Some of this exploration took the form of technology while other components were involved; such as the style of furniture being used.

Vision for the Information Technology Department

During my interview for the position of Director of Media and Instructional Technology, I was fortunate in that the then Director of Information Technology Services was a member of the interview team. He and I seemed to be on the same page from the outset. His perspective was that if I could tell him how many cars I needed on the highway, and how fast I needed them to go, he could build the highway to make that happen. I thought that was a great metaphor, and we continued to use it in communicating our plans with others over our time together. We worked very closely over my first two years in the district, and he made sure that Information Technology Department (IT) was supporting all of the Media and Instructional Technology Department (MITD) initiatives. Then, the fateful day arrived. The IT Director decided to retire. I was called into my boss' office, and informed that he had a new challenge for me, but he could not pay me any additional money. Yes, indeed I became the IT Director in addition to my current responsibilities. And, just to show you how stupid I can be: when the boss said he was going to move some of the IT responsibilities off to the Information Services Director I told him NO. I said, "If I am going to do this I want it all. I want to pull this wagon with one set of horses and see if we can make it even better." This was definitely one of those, be careful what you ask for you may get it moments. He agreed and gave me full control of both departments.

One of the biggest challenges of our IT department was working with an antiquated data center. We had severe cooling issues along with many servers that were considerably past end of life. We also had not made a strong move into the virtual server side of things. So, within two weeks of taking over the IT department I challenged the Senior Analysts to bring me a design for a new data center. I found out later that they had a big laugh that this new guy who was an instructional technology guy thought he would be able to get a new data center built. Well, twelve months later, we had a new state-of-the-art data center, and no one ever again questioned if I could deliver on my promises. I will talk more about this project when we discuss collaboration and communications later.

At the same time I made the challenge for the new data center, I also challenged the Infrastructure Team to give me a design for a high school with a 10 Gig core and a Gig to the desktop. Again, they thought I was crazy. Two years later we opened up two totally renovated high schools that met this new standard.

Just before I retired I met with the Infrastructure Analyst to discuss a new high school that the district expects to open in the 19-20 school year. For that school I am expecting them to need at least a 40 Gig core and Wi-Fi that can support 10,000 plus devices. As I told the Design Committee, if they open that school without having a device for every student on Day One, they will look really stupid and be totally out of step with the needs of the community. We have a new "medical pipeline" area that includes a new medical school at the University of Central Florida. In order to pull the parents, and therefore the students, the workers in this high paying area, the district must open the most state-of-the-art school yet to open in Florida.

Communications

Without communications, at many levels, projects may get completed, but no one will know what to do when they are. For instance, when we began thinking about interactive whiteboards, those of us in MITD began looking at the options. But, at the same time, we setup a technology mini conference to which we invited vendors who offered a variety of

> "It is simply impossible to become a great leader without being a great communicator."
>
> —MYATT,
> *FORBES LEADERSHIP,*
> APRIL 4, 2012

brands of the various technologies in which we were interested. Then we invited principals, teachers, and district level staff to come to that mini conference, and experience these new technologies. Later, we formed a committee of 37 stakeholder members to make the decisions as to which of the products we would actually purchase.

To be completely transparent, no members of MITD staff were given a vote in this decision. It was important that this be completely decided by those who would actually be using these products. The task for the MITD staff was to narrow down the choices for the interactive whiteboards, and then setup a "shootout" in which each company would present to the committee.

For the shootout, we divided the group up into elementary and secondary subgroups. Each group watched each product presentation in separate rooms. Elementary members saw SMART in their first presentation, and secondary saw Promethean. Each presentation was two hours long. After the first two-hour session, we provided lunch in a commons area, and then sent them back to their respective rooms for the second set or presentations. At the end of the second set of presentations, I told the group, "You have now seen what we consider to be the two best interactive whiteboards on the market. You are about to make a decision that will affect the students and teachers of this district for many years to come. Knowing what you now know, if you were going to purchase one of these products today, which one would it be? Please write your choice on the slip of paper provided to you, and drop it in the basket on the way out of the room. Thank you for spending your day with us and for assisting in making this vital decision."

Once everyone had left the room I sent someone down the hall to our Purchasing Department to ask one of their secretaries to come down, and count the ballots. I did not want anyone to ever be able to say that I or any of my staff had done anything to taint the decision made by this group of stakeholders. After counting the votes the secretary told me that they result was 31 to 6 for SMART. Wow! That was very decisive. We immediately notified the SMART representative, and began negotiating pricing for our implementation.

Next, the MITD staff held thirteen meetings in seven different locations across the district for others to come and hear the vision, and see some of the types of technology that we were considering. Of course, the interactive whiteboards were a big hit. We had limited funding at that point, so we set up a mechanism by which teachers could apply for funding to purchase an interactive whiteboard for their classroom. In their applications they had to give well thought out, meaningful learning goals as to how this new technology would be used in their classroom. "It would be great" was not acceptable.

Our next step was to develop a tiered plan for bringing all of these new technologies to all core subject area classrooms. This plan was shared with and approved by our Board. We determined that every classroom must first have a projector since nothing else could really happen with an interactive whiteboard or document camera without a projector. Then, each core classroom would be given a document camera. This was an easy sell since we were undergoing a huge professional development effort around writing, and the trainers were all using the document camera as a delivery tool. After document cameras were completed, we would move on to interactive whiteboards, and then audio amplification systems. Of course, at this same time, all new construction and renovations were placing all of the technology in those classrooms. Over the course of the next seven years, we worked diligently to accomplish this plan while visioning beyond that completion. Unfortunately, the recession of 2009 and other state and local funding issues kept us from being fully completed by the time of my retirement.

Anyone who has been involved with projectors knows that one of the key issues is the cost of bulb replacement. After our first major installation in which we did not use a projector that had networking capability, we saw just how many times teachers leave their projectors on overnight, and even over the entire weekend. Of course, this uses up a significant amount of the bulb life. At the time we began bulbs were approximately $250 each to replace. We determined that we had to do something to mitigate this problem. We needed to find a projector that we could control by setting times for them to turn on and turn off.

We searched for a projector with networking capability. Once we found the right projector at a price that we could afford, we began purchasing only that brand. This change also required close communication with our Information Technology (IT)/ Technology Services group. This group coordinates all construction that has any relationship to the overall network. We simultaneously located a ceiling mounting plate that allowed for a RJ45 network port to be included in the wiring configuration, and made this a requirement for ceiling mounted projector installations, whether in new construction, renovations, or retrofits.

At the same time as we were standardizing on the ceiling plates, we determined that we needed a wall face plate at which all technology connections could be terminated for the teacher's station. Again, considerable thought and communication with the IT/Technology Services group was necessary. We standardized on a teacher station that would be placed 12 feet to the left or right of the center of the interactive whiteboard with the station being on the side closest to the classroom door to the hallway. This determination was made after considerable conversations with teachers at all school levels. As it turned out, the elementary teachers wanted their instructional wall away from the door while secondary teachers wanted their instructional wall on the side of the room closest to the door.

As we were making the changes discussed above, we were also making changes in the layout of the instructional wall. We determined that a configuration that had four feet of corkboard then six feet of marker board, then the interactive whiteboard then another six feet of marker board, and finally another four feet of corkboard met the needs of most teachers. This change, along with the ones discussed previously, required a LOT of discussion with our architects. They had never encountered an Instructional Technology Department, so it tuned to the teachers who would also fight with them to get things right for the teachers.

As we began presenting our process at various conferences, other districts were astounded at the level of communications and collaboration that we had with both our IT department and our Facilities Department. In most other districts the Instructional Technology Department was not even a part of the facilities planning process.

Although we did not fully accomplish our goal as stated above, that did not keep us from visioning other new technologies for our students and teachers.

These included several iPad initiatives, 1:1 classrooms, expanded digital delivery systems, and increased digital content. All of these were closely developed by both departments while I was Director. Then in May of 2012 our new Superintendent decided that the district had taken advantage of me long enough, and decided to split the two departments back apart. Fortunately, the bonds had been built, and the IT staff were firmly ingrained in their thinking of how the two departments should work together. Also, the person chosen as the new IT Director was in favor of keeping that collaboration and communications open.

1:1 and Other Initiatives

As we moved into those new initiatives several issues surfaced that required close communications between IT and MITD. First was the issue of managing iPads on an enterprise network. This solution took months of research, and even at the time of my retirement was not fully functional. Neither IT nor MITD were ever totally onboard with the iPad concept. There were too many management issues, and we were simply too big to let them just run free. However, unfortunately, no other vendor had stepped up to develop and bring to market a device that could do what the iPad could do, so we just muddled along, and did the best we could.

In trying to work through the device issue we brought a team of Principals together. In many cases these Principals had asked about purchasing less expensive devices than iPads or other tablets that had recently come to market. As we talked through all of the things that we needed these devices to do, the unanimous decision was that a PC laptop was our best bet.

I know that many districts across the country have begun to use Chromebooks and other less expensive devices. We were a little reticent to go that way due to the demands of our state testing programs. The state Department of Education released minimum standards for testing computers, and we determined that with limited funding we could not afford to purchase anything that did not at least meet those minimum requirements, and could be easily managed on our network. Also, we provided our teachers and students with a very large amount of digital streaming content beginning back in the late '90s. We had to have devices that could run this content and perform numerous productivity functions at the same time. Our PC specifications were always significantly above the average for districts in our area.

First 1:1: Lessons learned

In putting together our first 1:1 project we chose a middle school with a strong, focused administrative team. We chose a middle school because our middle schools were getting a new English Language Arts (ELA) program with a full digital format. There was a book, but we wanted our students, in at least this one school, to go with the total digital format. The principal chose his seventh grade ELA team as our target team.

In order to get enough laptops for this program, we had to do what many of us do—scrounge. I had 25 laptops from one of my MITD training labs that were being replaced, so we donated those to this effort. The Principal dug up 25 at the school that were not being used for any specific purpose, and Title 1 allowed us to purchase 25 new units. We also scheduled one teacher into a computer lab for the two periods in which she taught seventh grade ELA. Now, that sounded like a plan.

One of my Technology Resource Teachers was assigned to this school for four days each week for the first nine weeks of the semester. He worked with the teachers to help them get comfortable with the management and use of the laptops. However, one classroom struggled from day one. We had forgotten that one of the carts of laptops was a mixture of three different brands of laptops. Wow, did that make a difference. Each brand had a different power brick. We had to color code each laptop, and then color code a corresponding slot in the cart to make sure that each laptop got plugged into the correct power brick. If they were not plugged in correctly, then they did not charge overnight, and therefore could not be used the next day.

Our second realization was that no matter how willing the teachers were to try this new approach, they just did not have the experiential background to do so. The Technology Resource Specialist spent a great deal of time just working on the management, not only of the laptops, but also of the class in general. Adding laptops in a classroom that does not already have strong structure with good classroom management does not make things better; in fact, it can make them worse, very fast.

> Our second realization was that no matter how willing the teachers were to try this new approach, they just did not have the experiential background to do so.

We also realized that the digital content had gaps in it. For instance, although students were supposed to be able to write in the program the mechanism for doing so was sorely lacking in some of the traditional word processing types of capabilities. So, we introduced the teachers and students to Microsoft's OneNote, and then later to the entire Office 365 suite.

The IT department was involved in every step of this process. MITD communicated the intent of the project, gave them the room numbers of the classes that would be involved, and the IT infrastructure group made sure that the wireless capability in those areas would meet our needs. In addition, when it came time for the first digital assessment, all of the seventh graders had to be tested at the same time. The school did not have enough computer capacity for this to happen. We determined that we needed 90 additional laptops in order to test all seventh graders at the same time.

We also realized that the digital content had gaps in it. For instance, although students were supposed to be able to write in the program the mechanism for doing so was sorely lacking in some of the traditional word processing types of capabilities. So, we introduced the teachers and students to Microsoft's OneNote, and then later to the entire Office 365 suite.

I called the Computer Support Analyst in the IT department, and told him that I needed to borrow some of the laptop testing carts for our 1:1 school to do testing. He located three carts (90 laptops), and had his staff move them to the 1:1 school the next day. Fortunately, we realized that these laptops had not been powered up since the beginning of the school year (that is another story all together). So, I had some of the MITD staff go to the school, get out the laptops, and turn them on. Lucky we did. These units had as many as 96 updates that needed to be downloaded before they could be used. That took a day and a half to complete. But, on Monday morning the testing went off without a hitch. In fact, one excellent result of this experience was that some of the teachers who were proctoring for the testing had never seen these students working on their laptops. The teachers were amazed at the ease with which these students moved through the testing.

As we approached the second year of our 1:1 initiative, we were fortunate enough to be given additional federal funds which we used to purchase new laptops. This additional purchase allowed us to complete the 1:1 project by giving the English Language Arts classrooms in grades six and eight the laptops needed for them to have a 1:1 environment as well.

Bring Your Own Device

We spent three years working on network configurations and upgrades in order to be ready for a Bring Your Own Device (BYOD) program. We leveraged the federal E-Rate program to purchase equipment and services to get everything ready. We spent a significant amount of time talking with teachers about this style of classroom environment. In the end it did not pay off.

Originally, we equipped our high schools first then our middle schools, assuming that those would be the students with the devices, and they would want to use them in their school work. However, the one thing that we overlooked was the students' ability to recharge their devices during the school day. Without such an opportunity, they simply did not want to use their devices for school work, and then not be able to have battery power to text and do other things after school; especially if they had a long bus ride home.

We had a great high school teacher with a highly engaged technology-based classroom. She began BYOD very early on, and became our go-to person when we need insights into how this would work. Coincidentally, she became our district's Teacher of the Year, and as such was given a very flexible schedule to go out to other high schools and talk with teachers about the whole realm of technology-based instruction used in her classroom. Still, there was very little buy-in for the BYOD program.

Elementary schools were excited about BYOD, but felt like they could not really do much with it since most of their networks were not upgraded. However, I developed a presentation in which I showed them that you can have a very active BYOD program using resident apps on your device. Students do not need to access the web in order to have meaningful activities with their device. For instance, if you have a class working on learning their multiplication facts, you can assign them homework to go home, and find an app that helps them learn those facts. The next day have each student share which app they found that they think is the best. After they have all shared, group them into groups of students who feel that the same app is the best for the class to use. You may get three to six groups. Then have each group develop a presentation about their app, and why it is the best. This requires a considerable amount of research into all of the other apps and serious critical thinking about how to best prepare their persuasive argument for their app. This could easily build into a week-long activity.

The Federal E-Rate Program

Since its inception, the federal E-Rate program had been coordinated by the Director of MITD. This trend continued during my tenure and beyond. Of course, this required a huge amount of cooperation and communication between IT and MITD. In addition, the Finance Department was included since they had to budget for the non-E-Rate portions of our projects, and the Purchasing Department assigned one buyer to work with us on these purchases.

MITD would scope out the plan as to which schools we would like to enhance classroom technology capacity, and then sit down with the IT department and review the plan. The IT folks would then survey those schools, and come back with a plan as to what needed to be done to meet the instructional needs for the future programs. The IT staff would make the list of necessary equipment, and coordinate with the MITD staff to put that list into the appropriate form to send out to bid. This process also included multiple meetings with the Purchasing Department. Occasionally those purchasing meetings could get a little heated since E-Rate requirements and our own purchasing policies did not always mesh.

This E-Rate purchasing process also required pre-bid meetings with vendors to make sure that they were fully aware, and would completely comply with the E-Rate requirements. We were bidding, at retail, approximately $10,000,000 in product. This usually came in at around $5,200,000 at bid pricing. This part of the process could take up to six months to complete.

After my first experience with an E-Rate bid, which was a disaster in that the vendors did not bid items in the order in which they appeared on the bid spreadsheet, it took us literally three weeks to resolve all of the issues with vendor submittals. For all E-Rate bids after that we locked the spreadsheets, and would not allow vendors to submit bids that were not fully submitted on the locked spreadsheet. It was amazing to me how many of the vendors would just choose not to bid on this amount of product because, "It is just too much work to do it your way." However, even with a limited number of bidders, we consistently received extraordinary pricing from those who participated.

Communications beyond IT[2]

Another department with which MITD had significant communications was our Facilities Department. Since buildings are designed two or three years ahead of actual construction, getting the newest technology into the new construction is not always easy. Again, this is where relationship building and communications are key. In this situation you have architects who have "done it this way for years", and project managers who are very comfortable with the way things have always been done. These two groups were real challenges.

When I arrived in Osceola County in 2007, we were about to open three new schools. When I walked into the first elementary school, I noticed that they had mounts for analog televisions on the wall. I asked why, and was told that was what we were using. UGH!!!! I then found out that we were using a media retrieval system that required coaxial cabling (approximately $100,000 worth) for the televisions and the control system cost approximately $85,000. UGH again. Since all of the wiring was already in the buildings, and the control systems were installed, it was too late to make a change. However, over time we changed out all of those televisions for interactive whiteboards, and retrofitted those schools with digital delivery systems that fed all digital content directly to the teacher's laptop, and then onto the interactive whiteboard. Once the Facilities Department realized that we did not spend any additional money to have this digital delivery system, they were content to make this change.

The only technology piece that I continually had to fight to get into new construction was the audio amplification systems. So many people just simply did not understand how important this system was to our students' capacity for learning. The teachers also strongly favored these systems as they did a lot to protect teachers' voices. Even teachers who would initially say, "I have a strong teacher voice", would admit that not having to push their voice as hard made life better for them too. At one point, I interviewed over 100 students from our two high schools that were rebuilt during my time in the district. When asked "Which of the new technologies in your classrooms makes the most difference for you?" the answer was consistently "The Audio Enhancement System. It allows me to attend for a longer period of time without getting as tired." Wow, that is a strong testimonial for these types of systems. In addition, our district has a very large English for Speakers of Other Languages (ESOL) population. The audio enhancement systems allow these students to hear the language more clearly regardless of the teacher's location in the room.

At one point our Purchasing Supervisor gave me a great suggestion. She said, "If you don't want to have to fight this battle anymore, simply submit this product to the Board as a Board Approved Standard." I did this right away, and from that point on, the audio amplification systems were built into the construction design and budget. Again, that relationship building and communication with our Purchasing Department staff paid off.

Another critical department for the Instructional Technology folks to have very close communications with is the Curriculum and Instruction Department. I know this statement seems to be one of those DUH comments; however, especially in larger districts, this just does not happen. The concept of all of us pulling the wagon in the same direction just does not seem to apply. I was fortunate enough to have a PhD in Curriculum and Instruction, and yet most of the district administration just thought of me as "the tech guy." In one significant meeting where the topic was the purchase of a progress monitoring tool, I had to remind the twenty or so people in the room that I was the ONLY one in the room with such a degree, not to mention 40+ years of experience.

Communication between the Information Technology Department, the Instructional Technology Department, and the Curriculum and Instruction Department are always challenging. First of all, there is an assistant superintendent and a director for each school level (elementary, middle school, and high school). In many cases the information that needs to be shared, and the decisions that need to be made can only be performed by those assistant superintendents. However, they are so overloaded with reflective visits and a host of other meetings and challenges that getting them into a one hour meeting is all but impossible. I have seen a number of significant initiatives never get off the ground because we just could not have THE meeting that needed to occur for the final go ahead. This kind of gridlock is really frustrating.

In theory, the Curriculum Department should drive all instruction and therefore all instructional initiatives, including those built around technology. In our district the only time that occurred was with iPads. The IT department was working very hard to get an enterprise management solution for tablets in general but primarily for iPads. Before that could even get in place, the Curriculum department purchased something like 450 iPads. As is too often the case, they had roll-forward Title 1 money, and just threw (in my considered opinion) it into an iPad "project." The only problem was the "project" was an empty shell. No one had a clue what they were really going to do with all of those iPads. As a result, six months later they were still sitting idle. In fact, it was actually over a year before they began to be used by students. The crazy thing in this situation is that the Instructional Technology Department was pretty much totally left out of the process even though we had built a list of apps for the iPads based on input from districts from around the country.

The above referenced situation is a perfect example of how not to operate. It is also an example of not having a long range vision and plan for technology that is embraced by all departments in the district. Had there been such a vision and plan, first, all relevant departments would have been aware of that plan, and second, whether or not this purchase was the right way to spend that roll-forward money would have already been answered.

In 2012 the Florida Legislature passed a statute related to digital education. That statute set out the parameters for a Digital Classrooms Plan (DCP) to be developed by every district. One great attribute of this legislation is that it required ALL stakeholders to be included in the development of the Digital Classrooms Plan. In our district that meant a committee of over 30 members. This committee was chaired by the Chief Information and Technology Officer (my boss), and the responsibility of pulling all of the components of the plan together, editing and submission was given to the Media and Instructional Technology Department. As you can imagine, getting all of the input needed from over thirty committee members was no small challenge

An overarching benefit of the DCP was that after it was approved by the School Board, it became the boiler plate by which all other initiatives were measured. If an initiative was proposed, we could now look at the DCP, and see if that initiative met one of the goals of that plan. If not, then we had some support for saying no to that initiative. One of the shortcomings of the DCP legislation, in my considered opinion, was that the funding for this program was sent to the district as a part of the general funding for the district. Although we had a DCP plan approved by the Board and the Florida Department of Education, we still had to have significant negotiations with our Chief Financial Officer to keep that funding segment committed to those goals set by the DCP committee.

> An overarching benefit of the DCP was that after it was approved by the School Board, it became the boiler plate by which all other initiatives were measured.

Again, no small task. For instance, the Chief Financial Officer (CFO) wanted to use some of the funding to pay the non-E-Rate portion of our phone and Internet bill. We actually had to get the Deputy Commissioner of Education on the phone to tell the CFO what he could and could not do with that money. And paying the phone and Internet bill was not allowable.

Communication with the Schools

For a district administrator who plans on initiating change communications with the school level, personnel is crucial. Too many district level people make up new programs, and "initiate" them without ever letting their school level personnel know what is going on. In MITD, as soon as we would have a new idea I would begin communicating with school level staff to determine if that idea had any merit for them. No idea is a good idea if no one wants to put it into motion.

I learned early on that good Principals have specific ideas for developing success in their schools. The only way that a district administrator can know what those plans are, in many cases, is to be in the schools on a regular basis. I have heard too many times, "I just cannot get out to the schools." Well, that, in my opinion, that is just not acceptable.

As a district administrator, if you are in your schools regularly, you will develop a level of respect and communications with principals and teachers, so that when you have an idea they will listen. Occasionally, I would present a new idea at our monthly Principal/Administrators' staff meeting. Sometimes, after I spoke I would sit down, and my email would start blowing up with principals in the room sending me emails to say, "I want to be a part of this new program. Please call me." Wow, that is a great feeling when they have that kind of confidence in your judgement to know that any idea I presented would be student-centered and beneficial to their achievement. Obviously, this does not happen overnight. But you have to start it by meeting them on their ground.

Collaboration

Collaboration, at any level, simply does not occur effectively if you have not taken the time to build relationships based on a mutual vision and trust. As a leader, your people must know that if you say it, you will do it. I have often cautioned young parents, "If you don't or can't do it, do not say it to your children." This goes for every situation. If you are a teacher, do not make threats or promises to your students if you are not absolutely sure that you can deliver on that threat or promise. If you are an administrator, do not commit to things that are out of your control.

> Once you feel that you have a certain level of relationship with various stakeholders in your work environment, you can begin to ask for help in making things happen.

On several occasions I was given the go-ahead to proceed on a project only to have that decision rescinded within a week. Based on that approval, I had already made plans, and communicated with principals only to have to call them and back up on my previous commitment. That is not a good position in which to be placed. Try to avoid such situations by waiting for a while before moving forward.

Once you feel that you have a certain level of relationship with various stakeholders in your work environment, you can begin to ask for help in making things happen. One of our middle schools was assigned a new principal three years ago. He was somewhat quiet, and it took several visits and walkthroughs at his school before he felt comfortable talking with me about a variety of issues. By the way, whatever anyone shares with you, unless they specifically ask you to communicate it on their behalf, you NEVER divulge who or where an idea for change came from to others. If you are in your schools frequently, you can simply bring up concerns without mentioning any particular school, and therefore holding the trust of those who told you about a situation. Everyone needs to vent sometime, and you have to allow them to do so knowing that you will "forget" where that idea came from if necessary.

So, you have good relationships built and you have an idea. I like to make an appointment and share my ideas face to face. I may give the other person a teaser like "Santa Claus wants to come see you." My folks know that means that I have come upon some money and want to share an idea for their school. If I get a positive response from the school administration then I proceed with communicating the idea to our IT Director and others who may need to be involved, including the assistant superintendent for that school division. Because I have built those relationships I already know that my idea will fit within the curriculum and student achievement goals for the school with which we will be working. A case in point is the 1:1 project mentioned earlier.

DR. MEL PACE served in a number of capacities over his 45-year long career. He has taught grades 1 through 6, been a school library media specialist, and served as a university instructor and administrator. His most recent position was as Director of Media and Instructional Technology for a large school district in central Florida. He also served as Director of Information Technology Services in a large district. He has been responsible for the visioning, planning, and implementation of numerous 21st Century technology initiatives. He is best known for his ability to get various groups and departments to collaborate and cooperate for the completion of intricate projects.

12

Driving Change in Workforce Management— Digitization is Key

Linda Misegadis and Rob Tibbs

As demands for technology in the classroom continue to rise, the administrative systems used by the workforce often get left behind. The culture of the workforce is changing, and school districts are faced with decisions on how to adopt technology throughout the school. Though new technology comes with costs, it also brings areas of efficiency, productivity, and visibility. How can technology bring a positive change to aging processes, and ultimately contribute to student success?

> How can technology bring a positive change to aging processes, and ultimately contribute to student success?

School districts across the country pride themselves and always want to shine in the educational community. Districts strive to be at the forefront with innovative ideas and solutions when it comes to educating our students. Technology provides opportunities for school districts with the necessary opportunities for that innovation. Through the years we have seem a transformation in the way students are educated, and this is mostly due to the advancement and use of technology in our schools. We have seen the revolution from using chalkboards to whiteboards and now the tech savvy smart boards that create an advanced and engaging classroom experience. Classrooms across the country have transitioned from textbooks to e-book readers eliminating the needs for students to lug books around. Teachers are embracing technology, and creating an environment for students with a variety of differentiated instruction methods to keep them alert, engaged, and constantly learning by leveraging apps and other technology advancements.

> All of this technology is being leveraged from a curriculum perspective, but many times back office and administrative tasks are not considered when looking at how school districts can better serve their students.

All of this technology is being leveraged from a curriculum perspective, but many times back office and administrative tasks are not considered when looking at how school districts can better serve their students. Antiquated processes are in all departments in schools; across the U.S. Human Resources, Payroll, and Finance are departments that are particularly afflicted with the need for better efficiency measures, but have little to no technology to help them accomplish these goals. Keeping track of employees is more than just about paying people correctly and on time. Keeping track of the time that employees work is more than just the traditional "clocking in and clocking out" perspective of workforce management. When a District understands what their workforce is doing, it opens a world a transparency and opportunity that drives better decisions.

Compliance

Compliance is another area that is often overshadowed by long-standing cultures within school districts. Manually tracking the hours that employees work on paper timesheets can create compliance issues. To be paid, employees can feel pressure to sign off on timesheets completed by supervisors, which can result in a labor-related lawsuit, particularly if there is a violation of the Fair Labor Standards Act (FLSA). An automated workforce management solution in which employees are responsible for punching in and out or recording their attendance, and managers are responsible for giving final approval, ensures all transactions are transparent and fully auditable. Employees must certify that their hours are accurate, and auditors can see who entered, edited, and/or approved each transaction.

Voluntary time is an artificial policy that pops up now and then when an employee works "off-the-clock", and often gets school districts caught in compliance issues. Though not done intentionally to withhold pay, many managers allow employees to volunteer their time not realizing it's a direct violation of FLSA regulations. This happens mainly when an employee is trying to save the district money by not running up overtime costs. It's a very noble act, but one that can come back to haunt employers should the employee become disgruntled.

Often there is a belief that because employees within the school district are classified as professional or salaried and salaried non-exempt employees, that they should not be required to track their time. There is concern from the administration that there will be resistance if they require their employees to be accountable for their time, attendance, and absences. However, media scrutiny over wasteful labor costs continues to plague the public sector including K-12 school districts. There has been an increase in Department of Labor audits within the public sector. Wage and hour audits are very costly, and can have a negative impact to employee performance and morale. With a proper approach to change management, there are simple ways to help transition employees from manual, paper-based processes to a full, automated workforce management solution.

> With a proper approach to change management, there are simple ways to help transition employees from manual, paper-based processes to a full, automated workforce management solution.

Washington County schools in the Southeast part of Utah provide education for 30,000 students in grades K-12. For a long time, the school district's process of collecting time and attendance information from employees was a purely a paper-based system. This made compliance to federal labor laws, such as FLSA and Family Medical Leave Act (FMLA), difficult due to duplicate data entry, errors, and limited reporting. A need for change was imminent, and they made a decision to move these manual processes of tracking time, and leave them to an automated solution. Once the transition took place, Washington County schools began seeing the benefits immediately.

To start, leave balances were now accurately reflecting on employees' paystubs. No longer were there forms to fill out to record leave. It's all recorded right in the system and available to see in real-time. Another advantage was the accurate accounting for FMLA eligibility and alerts for potential FMLA qualifying events that took some of the burden off the HR/Payroll staff for a more efficient process. Overall, employees are more confident that they are being paid accurately, and love the visibility into their time and leave balances.[1]

Overtime

School district operations are a must-have as schools could not operate without bus drivers, maintenance employees, food service, or child nutrition employees. These employees ensure the day-to-day operations go smoothly, and kids are transported safely, are in a comfortable, safe environment, and are properly fed throughout the day. Most employees providing these exceptional services are eligible for overtime. If a non-exempt employee comes in early or works through lunch, he or she might incur overtime by the end of the work week. With paper-based records, this would be difficult to catch until it's too late, and repeated instances like this can add up quickly. With a workforce management solution, however, K-12 leaders can set up automated alerts to indicate when an hourly employee is approaching 40 hours or is in danger of working overtime, so managers can plan accordingly—such as by sending the employee home early or adjusting the length of his shift. With a paper-based system, it would be impossible to get a handle on overtime or deal with it before it happens. But with an automated solution, users can spot key trends, and respond to potential problems quickly—before they get out of hand.

Per the *Journal News,* Nanuet school district spent $590,000 in additional pay for their building and grounds department within a school year.[2] An audit report revealed that overtime costs surged by 38 percent which is due in part to a lack of control and oversight. School districts across the country have been slow to adopt technology to assist with these efforts. Utilizing technology in these efforts can create accountability, efficiency, and the control Principals need to manage their workforce more effectively. While districts can quickly be under a spotlight from tax payers and the media, it is important to realize that principals' main focus is on student achievement. With manual,

[1] *Washington County Schools: Improving Efficiencies and Compliance While Reducing Costs Using Kronos® Workforce Management Solution,* 2016

[2] "Nanuet school overtime up 38 percent: NY comptroller", *The Journal News* January 8, 2016

inefficient processes, labor costs can skyrocket, and go unrealized when principals are not equipped with the tools they need to effectively manage labor costs, and ensure funding is secured for student success. By leveraging technology in the transformation of managing employee labor, it creates automation, efficiency, and complete accountability on the employees and school district.

Grant Funding and Audits

School districts are funded through a variety of sources, so it is important that districts control labor costs, and properly allocate funding. Common funding sources could be local tax revenue, state funding, as well as federal funding through grants and other initiatives. Because of the way school districts receive funding, they are at a high risk for audits. "The single biggest challenge in effective grants management is that many people don't record their time and effort on an ongoing basis," said Deborah Ward, a long-time grants consultant for K-12 school districts. "They might let that slide until the end of the grant period, at which time they are forced to go back and try to recreate this information. But that's an incredibly difficult thing to do after the fact." If school districts don't keep careful documentation to support the time and effort their employees spend on grant-funded projects, they could be forced to return funding in the event of an audit, Ward cautioned. Having the proper paper trail on how these funds are being utilized is critically important to ensure continued funding, as well as reducing any audit risks that may exist. It is important that school districts are fiscally responsible with every level of funding but especially federal grant funds.

> Because of the way school districts receive funding, they are at a high risk for audits.

Most grants or federally funded initiatives require controls and proper reporting of expenditures. With this comes record keeping. If school districts do not use technology for this endeavor, it could cost them millions. Recently, it was found that a large school district in the Northeast did not have adequate fiscal controls in place to account for federal grant funds that were expended during an audit period. The audit found that expenditures totaling over $100,000,000 from grant funds were either unallowable or inadequately supported. It was stated that the school district needed strong controls over personnel expenditures charged to federal grant funds. Being able to ensure that labor is being properly tracked and allocated to the proper grants or funding sources is critical to ensure compliance. It is critically important for districts to control costs and track funding so that more time and money can be spent in the classroom, and that the district does not lose funding. If school districts do not comply, it could result in a back pay of those funds as well as the elimination of any future funding. Most of these federal grant funds go to initiatives that directly impact student success such as tutoring and other enrichment programs.

Extra-Duty Time

More and more programs are being introduced in schools before and after school to keep the kids off the streets and in a safe environment. Extra duty and grants play a role in this endeavor by allowing school districts to fund additional support for students. Teachers may provide tutoring before or after school or allow students the opportunity for additional learning or extracurricular opportunities just to name a few. In order for school districts to provide this extra focus on student achievement, funding must be secured for these initiatives. One direct funding source for this is through federal grants. Reporting is a huge aspect of any grant fund, and not having technology in place to track the expense of these funds could be costly. It is important for districts to consider the implementation of a workforce management solution to track extra duty to create an efficient and auditable process to record the time worked and ensure proper recording on the backend. Without this in place, a lot of time is spent in administrative tasks tracking this and even then could not be enough for the record keeping requirements.

> It is important for districts to consider the implementation of a workforce management solution to track extra duty to create an efficient and auditable process to record the time worked and ensure proper recording on the backend.

Garland Independent School District (ISD) is a public school system in Texas with over 7,000 employees. They found tracking and paying employees, including teachers, who worked extra-duty time a difficult and tedious task. With hundreds of supplemental pay codes, it was nearly impossible to report back on labor allocated to grants. Weary of manually tracking extra duty, Garland ISD decided to automate this process with a Time and Attendance solution. All employees now clock in and out choosing job and pay codes from a dropdown menu that corresponds with their duty. By streamlining the process, Garland ISD was able to gain better visibility into these costs, and saw almost a 40 percent reduction in supplemental pay costs over three years. Now, at the touch of a button, the school district can run a report accounting for all labor costs associated with the state or federal grant funding supporting a particular extra duty job. Knowing where the dollars are spent just got a lot easier.[3]

Impacts of Absenteeism

Links to teacher absenteeism and student outcomes have been brought up in recent studies. In order for students to continue the evolution of learning and stay engaged and focused, teachers must be in the classroom. When teachers are absent, students are not learning and can easily become disengaged. Teacher absenteeism could be as a result of personal reasons, or even professional development reasons, or a combination of both. It is estimated that each 10 days of teacher absences reduce students' mathematics achievement by 3.3 percent of a standard deviation. Teachers on average work about 180-190 days per year. Ten days out of the classroom can be detrimental to student success, and this absence would contribute to a combination of reasons. School districts must look at this, and properly track this to ensure absenteeism is not a direct link to poor performance of their students and create unpreparedness in a student's future growth. Utilizing technology to track absences is a step in the right direction of providing principals and other curriculum leaders the information they need to track this data, and be held accountable to ensuring student success.

> It is estimated that each 10 days of teacher absences reduce students' mathematics achievement by 3.3 percent of a standard deviation.

[3] *Garland Independent School District Improves Productivity and Labor Cost Control with Kronos Solution,* 2014, https://www.uscommunities.org/fileadmin/hb/usc/Suppliers/Kronos/Garland_ISD_Case_Study.pdf

How effective are your district's substitute teachers? Do they have enough content knowledge to deliver instruction when a regular teacher is out? Are they skilled at classroom management or do they struggle to keep students on task?

There often can be a wide disparity in the skill level of a district's substitute teachers—but a workforce management solution can give K-12 leaders valuable insight into the effectiveness of these employees. By looking at workforce data, administrators can determine how a teacher's absence affected student behavior or achievement. For example, based on correlations between the days that substitute teachers work and corresponding disciplinary infractions, administrators can learn which substitute teachers seem most effective at keeping students focused.

Full-Time/Part-Time Analysis to Determine Healthcare Benefits

An important aspect of the Affordable Care Act (ACA) is that it expands health insurance coverage by changing the definition of a "full-time employee" to someone who works at least 30 hours per week instead of 40. To avoid penalties, employers with at least 50 full-time employees must offer coverage to at least 95 percent of these employees and their dependents. This Employer Responsibility Rule went into effect in 2015 for employers with 100 or more employees, and it went into effect in 2016 for employers with 50 to 99 employees.

The law requires K-12 leaders to pay close attention to who works an average of 30 hours or more per week, which imposes significant new data-tracking requirements on their school districts. The Employer Responsibility Rule contains various provisions and shortcuts for determining who is a full-time employee under the law, as well as how employees' hours may be counted. Substitutes may now be eligible for healthcare benefits under the Affordable Care Act. Historically, substitutes have always been considered a part-time, non-benefit eligible position. Their role is to fill in when teachers and other employees who have direct contact with students, are absent. Under the ACA, substitutes could be eligible for benefits if they work or exceed a certain hourly threshold as determined under the law. This could create additional expenditures for school districts as well as costly penalties if not properly tracked. Another component of tracking substitutes' time worked is how they are funded. Most districts leverage the funding source of that teacher to compensate the substitutes for the day they filled in. Doing this without technology can be a time-consuming and inefficient process. Some school districts will have substitutes allocate their time worked on the teacher's timesheet to provide ease of data entry and allocation of the correct funding source. While this creates some simplicity, when it comes to the ACA and FLSA, it can create challenges. It is important that all time worked for that substitute is recorded on one timesheet. This is to ensure compliance with the FLSA and now the ACA. However, ensuring the proper funding source is also equally important. Utilizing technology in this process creates ease of use for all involved as well as the assurance that districts can comply with all applicable laws, and be able to provide the level of reporting necessary.

Katy Independent School District (ISD) in Texas, one of the fastest growing school districts in the state, is home to more than 70,000 students and 13,000 employees. With a large workforce comes a greater need for substitutes including substitute teachers. After the Affordable Care Act was introduced, Katy ISD was concerned about capturing all substitute hours worked. A look-back period was needed to view on average how many hours' employees were working per week, and whether they were eligible for health care benefits. Originally, the Risk Management Department tried to calculate these hours manually, but it quickly became apparent that it was too labor-intensive.

Katy ISD turned to an automated report through their Time and Attendance solution to analyze the full-time/part-time mix as part of their compliance strategy. It only takes a couple of hours for the Risk Manager to analyze as opposed to a couple of days prior to automation.[4]

Emergency Response Plans

It is becoming more and more apparent that security in our schools should be a focus. Emergency preparedness should include knowing what students are present, but also which staff members are on premise at each school. Almost all districts have a process in place to track student attendance and tardiness. However, most districts do not have an

---

[4] *Katy ISD: Boosting Productivity and ACA Compliance with Automated Kronos Workforce Management Solution,* 2016

efficient and easily reportable process in place to account for employee attendance. As we see the need for emergency preparedness programs in place in schools, it is important to consider leveraging technology to track employee attendance so that in the event of an emergency personnel will know immediately what students and employees are present so they can all be accounted for. Workforce management solutions create this preparedness needed.

Conclusion

Labor is one of the largest operational expenses for any school district, but it's also the most important one. Creating an environment that allows employees and leaders to spend less time on administrative duties and more time dedicated to students provides an ideal experience for everyone. Keep in mind, too, that powerful and intuitive technology also helps recruit and retain employees.

LINDA MISEGADIS, *Public Sector Industry Expert at Kronos. Linda is a passionate, extensively experienced and goal-oriented industry consultant, K-12 Program Manager and former Payroll Director with over twenty years' experience in both the private and public sector. Linda is a Certified Payroll Professional, Certified Public Manager, and Certified Change Manager. She is the subject matter expert in state and local government, K-12 and higher education. Linda has proven expertise in driving efficiency and productivity through the evaluation of payroll, human resources and workforce management solutions. She is an effective change agent with a proven track record of facilitating change management initiatives both small and large scale. Previously worked at the City and County of Denver where she served as the Director of Citywide Payroll Operations and Administration. She successfully transitioned the City and County of Denver from a completely manual, paper based time management system to a state-of-art Kronos solution for all 13,000 city employees.*

ROB TIBBS *is a Solution Consultant for the Public Sector vertical at Kronos. He works on the Professional Services team aiding customers to access and design their Kronos workforce management* *solution. He has a strong public sector background specifically with 12 years in K-12 education.*

Rob comes to Kronos after previously working with the Jefferson County School District in Alabama where he served as the Director of Payroll. He successfully transitioned Jefferson County Schools from a completely manual, paper-based time management system to a state-of-the-art Kronos solution. Jefferson County Schools is the second largest school district in Alabama employing 6,000 full-time and part-time employees including substitutes.

13

TelePresence, Audio, and Video Conferencing: Why the Quality of Communication and Collaboration Matters

Jeff Billings

Located in northern Phoenix, Arizona, Paradise Valley Unified School District (PVUSD) has a history dating back more than one hundred years. Now with a mission of cultivating world-class thinkers, PVUSD knows that high-quality video and audio is critical to the success of both student education and to their business operations. Put simply, when one is able to communicate beyond text or audio, many more innate human traits are brought to bear, and authentic communication improves significantly. When communication improves, collaboration improves. When collaboration improves, problem solving capabilities improve.

If PVUSD is to cultivate world-class thinkers, high-quality, two-way audio and video conferencing becomes an important medium wherever and whenever possible. PVUSD has routed their TelePresence connections through the ultra high-performance networks of Internet2 and the National Lambda Rail for years. This in turn

> When one is able to communicate beyond text or audio, many more innate human traits are brought to bear, and authentic communication improves significantly. When communication improves, collaboration improves.

allowed remote communication and collaborations to occur throughout the world with but a heartbeat of latency in the signal. The natural flow of conversations, collaboration, and thinking is not disrupted by jitter or pixilation. PVUSD has been able to connect with world-class thinkers in world-class institutions across the world, literally.

Internally, PVUSD notes many successes through these sessions; from operations to teaching and learning. The human and cultural behavioral shifts are almost ubiquitous with now over 600 high-quality video endpoints, providing robust, quality communication when it matters. Conversations ranging from easy to hard are brought to life. Real collaboration occurs without the logistics of travel across PVUSD's 100 square mile domain. Visiting with universities, corporations, research enterprises and of course other K-12s are possible, all with a simple dial. The value of their real-time collaborations is significantly improved with sessions that embed workflows using their reliable, scalable, enterprise-quality video called TelePresence.

Series of Success Stories

This chapter dives into the practice of integrating TelePresence, specifically Cisco TelePresence, throughout PVUSD, a K-12 school district with 33,000 students. A series of success stories highlights the varied and diverse applications.

Quality Has to be There—Teachers

PVUSD has always cherished the value of communication as we collaborate to solve problems, celebrate achievement, and just live and learn in our journey of excellence. The use of TelePresence to support communication and enhance capabilities at a distance arose from the desire of educators to push for quality interaction, not choppy web video running 12 frames per second with periodic pixilation. That same desire pushed for sound quality that was essentially equivalent to being in the same room with someone, not the tinny noise accompanying someone lip syncing on a

> The use of TelePresence to support communication and enhance capabilities at a distance arose from the desire of educators to push for quality interaction, not choppy web video running 12 frames per second with periodic pixilation.

slideshow of screen refreshes. We all know it, we've all been there. Our teachers wanted quality so as not to disrupt the learning, not to interrupt the focus on the human side of the experiences that are inherent in synchronous communication. Could we get 30 frames per second or more of high definition audio and sound? Could we deliver rich communication, even being separated by distances of miles, tens and hundreds, even thousands of miles?

Doing so now enhances education at scale, at distance. We can develop human relationships, expand teachable moments to locations and distances that were impossible before. We would not have to commit distance education to only text or one-way, instantaneous communication. We could see the emotions of their eyes, their innate human expressions, the power of quality communication.

Thus, the path of TelePresence in PVUSD was born by teacher recognition of the power of quality communication. It became the mantra of PVUSD culture that the communication quality created for the boardroom should be driven to the classroom.

Ease and Reliability Has to be There

But, without ease of use in a technology, the technology will not be adopted. Without reliability in technology, the technology will not be adopted. Both ease and reliability are critical to introduce in any environment, perhaps especially true in the time-sensitive, instantaneous nature and people business of learning in K-12.

TelePresence takes advantage of two interfaces that have proven both reliable and easy. Specifically, the simplicity of a telephone number. One can give the average adult or child a telephone number, and the concept and application is immediately recognizable and achievable. About the same number of digits, an IPv4 address given to an adult, causes angst and confusion. Give any child or adult an email address with the "@" symbol and they got it, no problem. Both a phone number and email address can be used to make a TelePresence connection, whether it is a second grader or an adult. This fact has led to easy adoption in PVUSD.

With regards to reliability, the TelePresence architecture is built upon the same reliability of Cisco's globally-recognized Unified Communications System. This same Voice over Internet Protocol (VoIP) infrastructure carries not only voice, but now video in PVUSD.

Because of the high uptime, reliability has increased confidence by end users towards technology use and adoption.

QR Codes

A QR code is a two-dimensional barcode that allows for the generation and subsequent machine reading of information. Students as young as seven or eight become fascinated by the wonder of what happens when a computing device reads the code, launching for example a web browser to a specific web address.

PVUSD second graders determined that an experiment should be performed using QR codes and TelePresence. The students postulated that the resolution and quality of TelePresence would yield positive results, no matter the distance separating the sending camera and receiving display.

Figure 13-1.
QR code example

Armed with their brashness, they first tested using a relatively small experiment. They sent a secret QR code, one that would launch a website unique to their enjoyment, to a nearby middle school. The middle school students were able to read the QR code through the remote TelePresence screen and then describe the web page they were directed to. The second graders responded with excitement, joy, and laughter. So too, did the middle school students. This is simply the beauty of TelePresence—quality of life-like communication, collaborations, and relationships. And, proof of scientific experimentation, a learning process invaluable to K-12 students.

Armed now with one successful experiment, across several miles, the second graders contemplated their "moon shot." They wanted to dive deeper, go further, push the limits of all things enjoyable; from how far away could someone read their QR code using this media tool called TelePresence?

The PVUSD second graders had an opportunity to present to Harvard University, who was hosting the National School Boards Association (NSBA) conference. This was an experiment worthy of significance to a second grader. A distance of 2,630 miles, a big distance, even for second graders. Needless to say, Harvard and the NSBA were impressed when the experiment worked, and they saw it with their own eyes. The second graders were proud, almost boastful, as they knew all along it would work—see photo insert. Chalk one up for success in K-12 STEM (Science, Technology, Engineering, and Math).

Calculus III

A frequent challenge with high school enrollment in K-12s lies in classes that have to be cancelled due to insufficient numbers. In PVUSD's case, there were only a few students at each school who were qualified for the advanced mathematics of Calculus III. Due to this limitation, as well as the given state funding constraints, these students were facing the prospect of not being engaged at the appropriate level. Staffing a course with only a few students present is bad operations from a business perspective, and not sustainable in a public K-12.

PVUSD postulated, like the second graders, that the quality of TelePresence technology allowed us to think differently, to perhaps deliver teaching and learning in new ways. For the first time, PVUSD would deliver a TelePresence-enhanced, high mathematics course simultaneously to multiple high school campuses, each one bringing anywhere from one to five students. The instruction proceeded throughout the year, and the course was successful. No longer was PVUSD restricted to the walls of a classroom, to one campus or the other.

World Can Become Smaller, If We Want It To

Students and teachers, indeed our entire community, have obtained a perspective of the world that would have been impossible without TelePresence. The world became smaller, our differences became smaller, and our ability to understand one another became richer through national and global conversations. The conversations were enhanced because of the quality of the technical connection and signal. When conversations are conducted at a high quality level technically, collaborations and relationships evolve under the spirit of problem solving and celebration.

Internationally, PVUSD has developed relationships across the Atlantic and Pacific Oceans. From central Europe to virtual relationships with educators in Australia that resulted in in-person relationships. Over a series of communications, fifteen Australian educators, spanning the entire continent east to west, decided to come to PVUSD for over a week. Australia calls these visits walkabouts of sorts. There is much to be learned by cross-cultural conversations. Deep and rich dialog was exchanged through the relationship, all starting from the quality of TelePresence connections.

Nationally, PVUSD has connected with other K-12s; students-to-students, teachers-to-teachers. PVUSD also began a progressive outreach to better understand universities, the collegiate talent, and their research activities. How could we, as a K-12, better prepare our students for more advanced pursuits?

From private universities on both coasts, Stanford and Harvard, to public universities like University of Denver, University of Arizona, and University of Wisconsin—Madison, the relationships flourished with a simple TelePresence communication, and then advanced conversations resulting in authentic collaborations. No longer were these institutions simply names, logos, brochures, or websites. They became a part of PVUSD core DNA and culture. The quality of the communication mattered. Figure 13-2 demonstrates both national and international conversations and TelePresence sessions that PVUSD has had with institutions globally—the world is indeed small.

Training by TUKE
TelePresence is the core technology that brought a variety of relationships to PVUSD, nationally and internationally. Our strongest multicultural and multinational relationship was fostered by years of working and communicating between PVUSD and the Technical University of Kosice (TUKE).

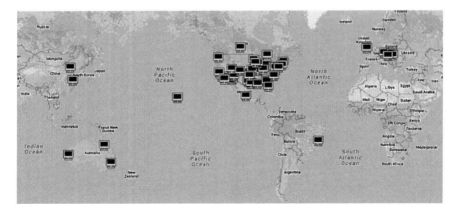

Figure 13-2. Global TelePresence Sessions by PVUSD

TUKE, located in central Europe, Slovakia, is well known for its technical aptitude. Perhaps nowhere is this more evident that in the technical underpinning of TelePresence and Cisco networking. One of the top five Cisco Networking Academy instructors in the world is at TUKE, and it was this instructor who taught PVUSD IT department staff.

Once a week for four hours each, over a period of four months, a series of training sessions occurred. These sessions were all conducted over TelePresence. The signal originated from Central Europe, traveling across the Atlantic Ocean and most of the continental United States to Phoenix, Arizona and back. Chalk one up for the ultra-performance network capacity of the Internet2.

Not once did pixilation or a dropped connection occur. Rather, uninterrupted learning via high-quality TelePresence was successfully demonstrated across very long distances and multi-hour sessions. From these early sessions, TUKE and PVUSD continue their relationship, including TUKE as the global Cisco Networking Academy sponsor of PVUSD.

Administrators and the Necessary, but Difficult Discussions

Seeing the whole picture, hearing the tones and inflections in voice, noting the facial expressions and body shifts, these all lead to rich communication available through the technology of TelePresence. Not just the instantaneous quality, but the signal throughout a communication session is consistent: a refresh rate equal to television video, a richness

Figure 13-3. TUKE/Cisco instructor in Central Europe looking back at PVUSD staff

> Quality in communication matters—reading body language, looking straight into eyes, listening and adjusting to oral arguments, complete with facial tone and simultaneous auditory response. ..TelePresence facilitates these conversations and allows a deep level of understanding and resolution, without the hassle of travel and logistics.

in voice that carries excitement, concern, break through humor, and all the goodness of the human-to-human interaction while communicating. So, too does quality matter when K-12 administrators need to have difficult discussions.

K-12 administrators deal with difficulties frequently. What's best for that one student, the parent who has a strong point, the teacher who is making a difference but needs to ensure compliance with all the laws, regulations and policies? How does a principal garner the support, who can they have a difficult discussion with, and how do they do it efficiently and effectively across PVUSD's 100 square miles of operations? TelePresence quality has proven instrumental in that regard.

Quality in communication matters—reading body language, looking straight into eyes, listening and adjusting to oral arguments, complete with facial tone and simultaneous auditory response. It is this level of quality that principals deserve and need to carry out their duties. TelePresence facilitates these conversations and allows a deep level of understanding and resolution, without the hassle of travel and logistics. Time matters to principals, as does the quality of communication.

Mandarin Grew to Four Years— UW Madison Helped PVUSD Develop It

Foreign language credit is required for being accepted into Arizona universities, and is a graduation requirement in PVUSD. Historically, this requirement was satisfied through successful completion of multiple years in French, German, and Spanish languages. However, demand has been increasing for the largest global language, Mandarin. Mandarin is particularly problematic in finding and retaining high quality teachers for the language. Additionally, a curricular program is difficult for K-12 to prepare as well as build. PVUSD contemplated a model of delivery similar to the success they had with Calculus III.

Specifically, could TelePresence be leveraged to teach Mandarin from one location, across multiple high schools?

PVUSD leveraged their connection with a nationally recognized university in global languages, specifically University of Wisconsin-Madison (UWM). An agreement was reached wherein UWM would provide their high school-based curriculum, training, and delivery of the content/course to PVUSD through TelePresence. Starting with the first year of Mandarin, this program has grown to four years of Mandarin, freshman to senior. It has also expanded to Mandarin now being introduced at not only the middle school, but also at the elementary level.

What was once a dream, Mandarin instruction in PVUSD is now a robust, multi-year program. PVUSD has developed a culture of world-class thinkers by connecting to and collaborating with world-class institutions.

Not to settle on one new global language, Hebrew is now taught at PVUSD. And University of Arizona has provided undergraduate credit to their students in the development and delivery of lessons to PVUSD elementary students on the Russian language, culture, and science history.

International Conference Presentation from PVUSD Classrooms

In the spring of 2014 PVUSD saw the need to develop a computer coding and a computational thinking K-12 program throughout the district. Rather than add new programs on top of programs, PVUSD chose to build computational thinking directly connected to English Language Arts and Math standards.

The Coding program has been wildly successful throughout the district, and is now being delivered K-12, with many avenues of success by students. Frequently, high school students teach middle and elementary school children the subject and practice of coding, all through TelePresence and shared screens. HTML, Javascript, and block coding such as Blockly and Scratch are taught and enjoyed by students on both sides of the TelePresence session.

Since the start of the global Hour of Code initiative, PVUSD has participated with tens of thousands of students during the month of December. It is quite remarkable to understand the experience of tens of thousands of students coding during the week. The logistics are complex, but totally worth it. Colleges of Education at University of Denver and University of Wisconsin-Madison have been willing observers of this experience, dialed into multiple classrooms from across the country.

An interesting application of TelePresence occurred in the winter of 2014-2015. Three of our elementary teachers leading PVUSD's Coding and Computational Thinking initiative were asked to present to a technical, international conference in Europe, all through TelePresence. Accounting for global time zones the PVUSD teachers presented at 6:30 on a fall, Arizona morning to a late-afternoon audience in Europe. The presentation subject was computational, analytical and model thinking by elementary-aged students using state standards. Imagine what is going on here. Elementary teachers presenting live over TelePresence to a technical, international audience in Europe. These types of experiences for teachers and for technical people throughout the world are not possible without the quality of TelePresence. K-12s can welcome the world into their classrooms, and the world can welcome K-12s. Everyone benefits from quality conversations.

Brigham Young University Undergrad in Computer Science Tutors PVUSD Student on Coding

There is a problem nationally, and it exists in PVUSD as well. Specifically, females are not well represented in number of the STEM fields in general, and computing fields such as Information Technology and Computer Science, in particular. In an effort to combat this underrepresentation, PVUSD has a Women in Information Technology initiative, wherein amongst other activities, female undergraduate students are called upon to model STEM thinking to PVUSD's young women.

Figure 13-4 depicts a former PVUSD graduate, now at Brigham Young University, tutoring a PVUSD student. Here the tutoring continues with discussion on logic functions as coding constructs. From a dorm room in Salt Lake City to a classroom in Phoenix, TelePresence brings in quality collaborations. The one-on-one modeling by a Computer Science university student to an upcoming PVUSD young woman is a powerful human relationship, all enhanced through the quality technology of TelePresence.

Center for Teacher Development

One of the best methods of developing teachers is simply through the observation of master practices and master teachers. One of the challenges with observation has always been in both the logistics and time commitment of going to and from locations to observe. TelePresence breaks down the distance barrier, thus saving considerable time across PVUSD's 100 square miles. The second challenge with observation is that as soon as a guest comes into the classroom, the dynamics between the teachers and student within begin to change.

> One of the best methods of developing teachers is simply through the observation of master practices and master teachers.

In an attempt to offset these challenges, PVUSD began to explore a model using their TelePresence infrastructure. Dialog with parents and teachers established the need and permission. Technical analysis identified high quality, pan—tilt—zoom cameras and omnidirectional microphones in the ceiling. Under the guidance of instructional coaches, teachers from one school could observe the practices of a master teacher, live, without disrupting the classroom and without the wasted time of travel. The Center for Teacher Development program has been very

Figure 13-4. Tutoring BYU student to PVUSD student

successful, with specific observations scheduled for specific ongoing practices. Several local and out of state observations, some graduate schools of education have likewise observed and discussed through follow-up conversations.

Now on the Smart Phone and Chromebook

PVUSD started with approximately 55-inch display TelePresence units, resulting in effectively creating small conference rooms in which to converse. As technology has progressed and business cases increased, so too has the journey into high quality conversations across distances, TelePresence.

PVUSD now enjoys a variety of footprints in their TelePresence infrastructure. They have deployed large 70-inch displays, units capable of output through HDMI for very large projection. Similarly, the evolution deploys endpoints with a small footprint functioning as a video phone, to desktop display footprints similar to a 24-inch computer display.

Rounding off their fleet, TelePresence through the Jabber app (IOS and Android) is now seeing deployment on SmartPhones. All clients, no matter the footprint, are tied into the enterprise infrastructure. PVUSD now has one number or contact, multiple device footprints, all with the same purpose—quality conversations no matter the location. A recent addition, brought on by Android operating on Chromebooks, promises to bring even more integration in PVUSD, with a large fleet of over 30,000 Chromebooks.

Conclusion

The value of TelePresence in K-12 had been highlighted through this series of successful applications. Breaking down the challenges in communicating and collaborating across distance, across state and national borders, amongst differing cultures, continues to be a wonderful Journey of Excellence. Connecting to the world has allowed PVUSD to consider what it takes, and then to take steps towards their pursuit of cultivating world-class thinkers.

JEFF BILLINGS, *Information Technology (IT) Director at PUVSD, has been with the district for 17 years. Mr. Billings operated his own hazardous waste remediation company for 15 years, yielding several U.S. and foreign patents. He has published peer-reviewed scientific papers, presented nationally and internationally, in person and virtually. He became involved with education through selection as the first Arizona Education Association's, Business Partner of the Year. Since 2000, he has been the IT Director of PVUSD in Phoenix, Arizona. There, he has also served as the IT Policy Advisor to the Arizona Department of Education and to the Governor's Office as the K-12 representative on the Arizona Data Governance Commission.*

14

Scaling Flipped Learning

Jon Bergmann

"We don't just want to flip classes; we want to flip schools."
—Ignacio Romero, MT Groupo, Spain

Flipped Learning at its core is a very simple idea. Students interact with introductory material at home prior to coming to class. This usually takes the form of an instructional video created by the classroom teacher. This replaces the direct instruction, which is often referred to as a lecture, in the class. Then class time is repurposed for a variety of tasks such as projects, inquiry, debate, or simply working on class assignments that in a more traditional class would have been sent home. This simple time-shift is transforming classrooms across the globe.

The flipped learning movement has been growing significantly over the past number of years. In February 2015 Project Tomorrow released the results of the Speak-Up survey. They found that 28 percent of administrators say that flipped learning is having a significant impact on transforming teaching and learning in their districts. Seventeen percent of elementary schools, 38 percent of middle schools and 40 percent of high schools are implementing it with "positive" results.

Dr. Richard Talbert surveyed the number of scholarly papers about flipped learning which is illustrated in Figure 14-1. Dr. Talbert postulates that the dramatic increase is attributable to the publication of *Flip Your Classroom: Reach Every Student in Every Class Every Day.*

Not only has Flipped Learning increased in practice in the United States, it is also growing exponentially internationally. Flipped learning as an

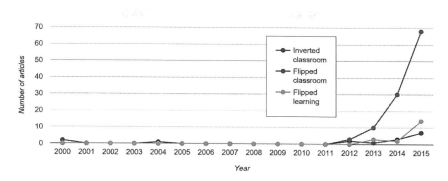

Figure 14-1. Number of peer-reviewed articles containing
FL terms in title or abstract

educational methodology is growing, and will not soon go away. The
Flipped Learning Global Initiative (FLGloal.org) has named flipped
research fellows from across the globe. The Lead Research Fellow is
Dr. Caroline Kurban, who oversees flipped learning at MEF University
in Istanbul, Turkey, the first fully flipped university in the world. Join-
ing her team are professors from Australia, Spain, Taiwan, China, Mexico, and the United States. The Initiative also has a group of Master
Teachers who hail from all over the world. Flipped Class conferences
have popped up all over the world. In the past few years, I have had the
unique privilege of crisscrossing the globe, helping educators flip their
classes. I have personally visited flipped classes in Iceland, the UK,
Korea, China, Taiwan, Mexico, Argentina, and Spain. I have seen the
promise of flipped classrooms, and I have also seen where flipped
learning has struggled.

One of the great strengths of the flipped class movement has been
its grass roots nature. It is a rare school that I visit where there aren't
one or two teachers flipping their classes. Most teachers who have adopted the model, have adopted it in small pockets. It is great when
teachers feel freedom to innovate and do what is best for their students.
This bottoms-up approach has been powerful. However, bottoms-up
innovation can sometimes reach a point where it will not flourish unless
there is thoughtful and systemic change.

This past year I worked with a group of about 60 teachers from a
variety of schools in New York state who were learning how to flip
their classes. I visited them four times during the year, and got to know

their successes and challenges. Several of the teachers had great results, and said they could never go back. Others faced significant challenges which left them frustrated. They are convinced that flipped learning works, yet they were discouraged. The majority of their issues would be resolved if their schools and districts would think systemically about flipped learning.

Though flipped learning can be executed by one teacher in a class with little support from administrators, it is not ideal. It is time for schools, and especially school leaders, to set up systems which will ensure maximum success for teachers. Flipped learning has reached the tipping point, and it is now time to think about it on a larger scale. Flipped schools now exist in pockets around the world, and when a whole school adopts the model, the resulting synergy is truly phenomenal. I have worked with most of these schools, and the transformations are remarkable, and should be emulated. For schools to scale, flipped learning has seven distinct things which need to be addressed.

Teacher Buy-in

Getting teachers convinced that they should embrace change is critical to scale flipped learning. If teachers don't see the value in the model, the roll-out will stall. I have seen teachers sabotage flipped learning by a variety of means. In one school approximately a dozen teachers were flipping their class with good results, and a small group of teachers started rallying students against the method. These teachers feared change, saw the method as a threat, and attempted to squelch the change. Their efforts stalled change, and created animosity between teachers. This underscores the necessity of getting all teachers to at minimum support the teachers who are embracing change. As I have worked with schools, I have found some successful ways to get teacher buy-in.

Start With a Few
It is not wise to launch a whole-school flipped initiative all at the same time. Not every teacher is ready to flip right away. Begin with a small group of dedicated teachers who are ready for change.

Make Sure Teachers Understand the Model
I have met so many teachers who learn that I am a pioneer in flipped learning, and immediately tell me why flipped learning won't work in

their situation. They mention access, student lack of homework completion, technology hurdles etc. But what is almost always clear is that teachers have an incomplete idea of the flipped class model. I have found that once the model is explained well, and presented in a such a way that isn't overwhelming, most are quick to embrace it. It is best if the model is well explained to all faculty so that all teachers can at least support those who will be the pioneers at their school.

Who Should Be in the Initial Group?

I worked with a school that got their initial cadre of flipped teachers together, and when the principal introduced them to me, I turned to the principal, and told him we had the wrong group. I observed that all of the teachers were twenty-something teachers who seemed good with technology. I told the principal that we needed a few teachers with gray hair. It is imperative that your initial cadre of flipped teachers include somebody who is an older teacher, who is well respected by the staff, and ideally, is hesitant about technology. Because if this older, techphobic teacher can flip, the rest of the staff will conclude, "If he/she can do it, I can do it!"

What Subjects Should the Cadre Teach?

Should a school focus on a specific content area first? Though this may seem like a good strategy, it is more important to start with the "right" teachers; the ones who will successfully implement the program. Every time I share with a leadership team I ask them to identify the "right" teachers, and they always can come up with the list. However, if there is one department which is more ready for change, it is sometimes smart to get flipped focused there. The fear I have with this approach, though, is that the teachers in the other departments might see flipped as something just done in a specific content area, and not see it applying to their subject area.

The Best Way to Spread the Flipped Class

Since you want to spread the flipped model beyond your initial cadre, the best way to do this is to have the initial cadre flip well. Give them the tools and support for them to successfully implement the model. I have worked with a group of thirty teachers from one school over the past two years, helping them implement flipped learning. In my most recent visit, I had a chance to visit classrooms, and share with teachers who were not in the cadre. I was pleasantly surprised that flipped has spread beyond the initial group, and now flipped learning has infiltrated the school. The teachers in the cadre implement well, and now the rest of the faculty is jumping on board.

How to Influence Teachers

In 2007 Dr. John Diamond, an education professor at Harvard University, did a study of what influences teachers to change. Figure 14-2 summarizes his findings. He concluded that teachers' primary reason for change was listening to other teachers.

Secondarily was internal motivation, and third was students. Note how far down on the influencers was the principal. Maybe the secret to change is to get teachers to think the flipped class is their idea, and then let it spread.

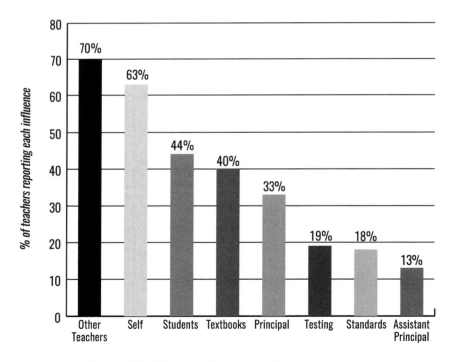

Figure 14-2. Teacher's reports of the influences on their teaching strategies

Flipped Learning Is Not That Radical

For those who fear giving up control of content and curriculum, realize that flipped learning is actually a balanced learning approach. The teacher can still hold onto content while at the same time enabling a more student-centered class. The idea of simply recording a teacher's lectures is not that big of a step for a teacher who is used to presenting content. We forget that students don't know what they don't know, and teachers do. There is a reason departments of education have curriculum guides. Many very smart people have spent countless hours determining what students need to know, and are able to accomplish. Let's combine student-centered education with the fundamentals from our curriculum guides. I like to think of this as a continuum.

When I say we need balance, I feel class time should be a balance between the two extremes. But how do we do this?

If we rethink the continuum, I think flipped learning fits right in the middle. It creates space for traditional learning, and gives time for students to take more ownership of their learning.

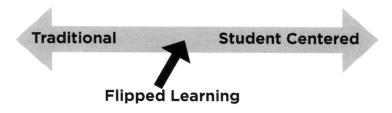

One reason many educational movements have gone poorly is that we have swung from one extreme to the next. Most teachers I know are uncomfortable with the extremes, and are unlikely to embrace fully student-centered classrooms. Flipped learning is a way to foster greater student ownership of learning while at the same time valuing and encouraging curriculum.

Technology

Technology infrastructure matters. If there is inadequate technology, flipped learning is difficult to implement. All of the large-scale flipped learning implementations I have seen around the world have had to invest significantly in technology infrastructure.

Integration

It is important to think through what technology is best suited for your school or district. When I consult with schools starting on this journey, I insist on spending time with their information technology (IT) staff, discussing their individual technological infrastructure. Integration is the key. Which tools a school chooses should integrate with existing technology in each school's infrastructure. They need to address questions such as:

- Is this tool compatible with our single sign-on platform?
- Does this tool integrate with our learning management system?
- Does this tool integrate with our student information system?
- Does this tool work only on all devices provided by the school, or is it a tool which students typically have access to at home? Since many students now access information on mobile devices, it is imperative that any tool be mobile-friendly.
- Which tools are the best for the hardware infrastructure of our school? The best tools for a personal computer are different than for a Mac, and still different for a Chromebook.

These and many other integration questions should be answered before bringing flipped learning to scale.

Video Creation

There are many ways to create flipped videos. Teachers can use their smartphone, a document camera, or screen capture software. Choosing the right suite of tools makes a big difference in the success of any flipped learning initiative.

Video Hosting

Where will the videos be stored? Should a school host their videos on YouTube, TeacherTube, Google Drive, or in their learning management system? Each of these decisions is best made systemically. It is not efficient if teachers are hosting their videos in different locations.

Learning management systems (LMS)
I have seen cases where one school has one teacher using Edmodo, another Schoology, another eChalk, another Google Classroom, and yet another Moodle. Though each of these tools is good, having so many options creates confusion amongst the students, teachers, and staff. Professional development also suffers because technology trainers must work on any or all platforms. To that end, each school should support one learning management system.

Workflows
When I was Lead Technology Facilitator at a school district in Illinois, it became abundantly clear to me that I needed to develop simple workflows for teachers. If a teacher has to use one program to make a video, another one to add in interactivity, and another to host a video, then the system complexity discouraged teachers from implementing flipped learning. I constantly thought about workflows that required fewer clicks and less technological expertise. When I work with schools and districts, I customize the flipped workflows with simplicity in mind. So, keep it simple! Fewer clicks! Make flipped learning simple and carefully think through your workflows.

Bandwidth and Wi-Fi Access
The world is becoming increasingly mobile. Mobile devices are the future of Internet access. This is especially true in the developing world where individuals are leapfrogging wired infrastructure, and building everything for mobile devices. Creating a robust wireless network is a must for every school. This represents a significant investment, but it is necessary if flipped learning is to be implemented well.

What Happens When Technology Fails?
One challenge I hear over and over from teachers is that too often school-provided devices don't work. There is nothing more frustrating for a teacher than planning a lesson which requires technology, and then the technology does not function. Unreliable devices need to be jettisoned, and replaced by devices which turn on quickly and

function without issues. Teachers are also frustrated with a lack of access to school devices. There may be an iPad or Chromebook cart, but since they can't get timely and regular access to the devices, they quickly give up.

I realize that upgrading the technology infrastructure requires an outlay of money, but in this digitally connected world, it must be a priority in schools. So if you want to implement flipped learning with efficacy in your school or district, you must invest in the technology necessary for flipped learning.

Pedagogical Change

Educational researchers have been studying learning for a very long time. In 2005, Patricia Cross wrote an article entitled "What Do We Know About Students' Learning and How Do We Know it?". She summarized this with seven principles:

1. Good practice encourages student-teacher contact.
2. Good practice encourages cooperation among students.
3. Good practice encourages active learning.
4. Good practice gives prompt feedback.
5. Good practice emphasizes time on task.
6. Good practice communicates high expectations.
7. Good practice respects diverse talents and ways of knowing.

These seven principles mesh very well with flipped learning. They probably come as no surprise to experienced educators, but when we are honest, too much of what happens in schools does not reflect these principles. Instead, many classes are passive, and students spend too much time listening to teachers present content.

Dr. Cross goes on to state: "Active learning is the grand meta-principle." Learning science tells us that active classrooms are the key to learning, and yet too many classes fall flat. This principle was recently confirmed during an interview I conducted with Dr. Baohui Zhang from Shaanxi Normal University for the "Flip Side Radio" show which I host. In our conversation, I asked, "Why does flipped learning work?" Dr. Zhang replied simply, "It is because students are more active in their classrooms."

Are the vast majority of classrooms active places of learning? Are students engaged, interested, collaborating, and challenged? The sad fact is that too many classrooms are teacher-centered, focused on information transfer versus active places of learning.

So how can schools and systems scale flipped learning from the perspective of pedagogy? Below are few suggestions:

- ◼ *Mindset change*—For a large scale adoption of flipped learning to occur, teachers must believe that active learning is superior to passive learning. Mindset change is the most critical step. Without an underlying mindset change, flipped learning will have little impact.

- ◼ *Collaboration and teaming*—The best flipped examples I have observed have been when groups of teachers plan and implement flipped learning together. Administrators should identify key teachers who have made the mental switch and support them through the flipped learning transformation. Make flipped learning teams a part of the fabric of your school.

- ◼ *Model flipped learning*—If flipped learning is good for students, then it is an even better idea for professional development. When schools flip their professional development, teachers will themselves be engaged in an active learning experience.

- ◼ *Actually do it*—I have met many teachers who say they believe in active learning, yet don't practice it. Maybe it is time for administrators to give reluctant teachers a gentle nudge while providing the support they will need to change.

Ultimately, the goal of flipped learning is for teachers to create active places of learning.

Let's not just flip classes; let's flip schools! Start having those deep conversations about pedagogical systems and practices.

Teacher Evaluation

During my twenty-four years as a classroom teacher, I was evaluated many times by administrators. The majority of these evaluations consisted of the principal sitting in my class, and watching me "teach." He or she took notes, plugged the information into a rubric, and then later we sat down and discussed how things went. Since most of my class was a teacher-centered presentation, I strived for great presentations which engaged my students, inspired their curiosity, and sparked rich questioning. Later, during our evaluation meeting we would discuss the lesson, how I could have improved, my goals for the year, and how I planned to make myself better. In many ways, the focus of the conversation focused on delivery of information: how I could be clearer, how more students could understand the content, and how to engage the unengaged.

But then I flipped my class, and direct content delivery happened outside of class. The students accessed the flipped videos on their own time. The typical evaluation systems didn't fit into the traditional rubrics.

During my second year of flipping my class, I was up for a review. My principal Del Garrick came in for his yearly evaluation. He sat down to watch the class, and he didn't get what he was expecting. Instead of a teacher-centered presentation, kids were actively engaged in learning from the start, with what appeared to be little prompting from me. As I was interacting with kids, I turned to Del, and invited him to take part in helping some students with an experiment. He became an active part of the learning community, and experienced the class as a student, and also as a teacher. When we met later, our conversation was not about how I could present content more explicitly, but rather, about how flipped learning leads to active students. Del told me that the rubric didn't apply. Then he added: "I get it. Kids are active, engaged, and learning. Keep up the good work."

A few years ago I had a chance to chat with Greg Green, the principal of Clintondale High School, the first fully flipped school in the world. We discussed how he evaluated his teachers, and he told me that before they flipped, 80 percent of class time was teacher-centered, and 20 percent was student-centered. After the school had flipped, the numbers flipped. Now only 20 percent of class time is teacher-centered, and 80 percent is student-centered. He then built the 80-20 rule into his evaluation system, and he expects that classes will have much less teacher talk-time and much more student activity time.

> As a school expands flipped learning, it is imperative that the evaluation systems get redrawn.

As a school expands flipped learning, it is imperative that the evaluation systems get redrawn. Below are a few evaluative areas which should be addressed when you scale flipped learning:

- ◼ *Pre-watch the flipped video*—Since a flipped class hinges on students doing the pre-work, it will be best if the principal views the same video as the students before observing a class.
- ◼ *Evaluate the flipped video*—Since students consume content via a flipped video, there is a need for administrators to evaluate the videos teachers create. Videos should not just disseminate information but should also have built-in interactive elements which engage students.
- ◼ *Evaluate class activities*—Does the in-class activity match the purpose of the lesson? How engaging is the in-class activity? To what extent are students on task and learning?
- ◼ *Evaluate teacher-student interactions*—What is the quality of interactions between the teacher and his or her students? To what extent does the teacher get to every student? Are the questions differentiated for students with varied abilities? Does the teacher guide instead of tell?
- ◼ *Evaluate student-student interactions*—Students all over the world say they love flipped classrooms because of how much time they get to work together. What is the level of student-student interactions? Are they probing, questioning, and solving problems without teacher assistance? Flipped classrooms transfer ownership of the class to students, so in an exceptional flipped class, you will observe deep student conversations.
- ◼ *Expect noise*—Flipped classrooms are not usually quiet. They are busy and active. Don't expect to find kids quietly sitting in desks.

Learning Spaces

Before I flipped my class, students faced the front of the room. The focus of the room was on the screen and a whiteboard. I used Power-Point as a way to display slides, and used the whiteboard to work out chemistry problems. I, the teacher, was the focus of the room. But when I flipped my class, I got away from the front of the room. No longer was the purpose of the room content dissemination; instead, the purpose was active learning. I rarely turned my projector on because students were busy learning in the class.

As I realized that the focus of the room was no longer on teaching, but rather learning, I rethought many things, including how to best utilize space to accommodate teaching with the flipped classroom in mind.

Rearrange Your Furniture

First, I simply rearranged the furniture. Instead of the tables in nice neat rows, I arranged the furniture in a way that fostered student collaboration, movement, problem solving, and exploration. Rearranging the furniture may seem like a small thing, but it led to powerful learning outcomes for my students.

Interactive Whiteboards

After about a year of flipping my class, I received a grant for a Smart-Board. I was excited to get it not because I wanted a better presentation station, but because I wanted a place for students to interact with digital content. It was mounted on the side of the room, and it quickly became "the" place for students to work. They loved being able to discuss science and interact with online simulations together on the big board.

Analog Whiteboards

As I have visited flipped classrooms across the world, one observation I have had is that there is never too much whiteboard space. Students love to interact with markers and whiteboards. Since a flipped class is by definition an active place, then have as many whiteboards as possible. You may even want to invest in whiteboard paint and make entire walls into marker space.

Purchase Collaborative Furniture

And as your flipped classrooms expand to more and more teachers, it is likely time to rethink standard school furniture. Standard school furniture's purpose is for students to sit and take notes. It is not designed often designed for collaboration and exploration. Most educational furniture manufacturers now offer furniture which allows for greater interaction and collaboration. These are a worthwhile investment. However, let me tell one story of caution. A few years ago I visited a major university which had bought the latest in collaborative furniture for their classes. They spent hundreds of thousands of dollars on this upgrade. But as I visited the classrooms, virtually every professor had put the furniture in nice neat rows so that they could teach in the traditional manner. What the school had not done was help their professors make the mindset shift to active learning. Buying furniture will not help unless the mindset change has not happened first.

Provide Quiet Spaces in a Noisy Room
Flipped classes are busy places, and the volume of the room is typically higher than a standard classroom. For some students, this can be over stimulating. Many introverted students and students with ADHD might need to have quiet places to ponder, think, and process. Ideally, a room could have a glassed in quiet space for students to work. However, this is usually very cost prohibitive. A way to give students a quiet space in noisy classrooms is to purchase noise canceling headphones.

Parent Buy-in
Sometimes students don't always communicate with their parents accurate information about what is happening in school. If a child is struggling in class, they often look for something/someone to blame. Flipped learning may be cited as a cause for those students struggles. Some students will tell their parents: "My teacher is not teaching anymore." Others will say: "I can't learn in that system." In addition to this is the reality that for most parents, the idea of flipped learning is new, and some may be skeptical. Thus, it is imperative to communicate to parents why your school is embracing the flipped model.

Creative Communication Strategies

Flip Your Back-to-School Night
Have teachers flip back-to-school night (curriculum night) by creating short videos for parents to watch before the event. Then during the event, have a discussion about the benefits and implementation of the model.

Host a Traditional Meeting
I worked with a school which embraced flipped learning, and they set up a series of meetings with parents. During the parent meetings, they explained what flipped learning is, why they chose to implement it, and how to help students.

Flip Community-School Meetings
School leaders often meet with parents and community leaders. Instead of making content presentation the focus of the meeting, flip the meeting. Create a short video about with the key information and then go deeper during the face-to-face meeting.

Letters/Email/Newsletters Home
The key is to find ways to inform parents about the new model, and as they become aware and informed, they will become your strongest supporters. This is no different than if a school changes the bell schedule or the bus routes. Get the larger community behind you. Many schools and teachers have used my post entitled "Five Reasons."[1]

What Message Should You Send in These Communications?

Now that you have a communication strategy, what should be the message you send about flipped learning?

Greater Interaction
Tell parents that teachers will spend less class time giving information, and more time helping students with difficult concepts. Their kids will have more one-on-one time with their teacher. This is, by far, the most powerful message to send to parents. All parents want is for their son or daughter to have more personal attention from their teachers.

Active Learning
Parents all remember being in "that class." The one where they either couldn't follow the teacher, or were bored out of their minds. Let them know that flipped classrooms are different. They are active places of learning, and students will be more engaged in class.

Other Considerations
Make sure you also address the following foundational questions:
- How will students access the content?
- What expectations are there for families regarding technology?

---

[1] http://www.jonbergmann.com/five-reasons-parents-should-be-thrilled-their-child-is-a-flipped-class/

- How long will the videos be?
- How many flipped videos do they anticipate students watching per week?
- Why is the school embracing the flipped model?

In summary, communicate, communicate, communicate. You can never communicate enough. Be clear, be consistent, and be relentless.

Summary

Flipped learning is best implemented at scale when it is thought through systemically. The method is working for teachers and students, and now it is time for it to work on a large scale with entire schools. Answering the above questions and thinking them through will enable schools to go flip with efficacy.

Bibliography

Bergmann, Jon, *Breaking Through the Biggest Barrier to Flipped Learning* (Bam Radio Network, 2015), http://www.bamradionetwork.com/the-flip-side-with-jon-bergmann/3961-breaking-through-the-biggest-barrier-to-flipped-learning

Cross, Patricia, *What Do We Know about Students' Learning and How Do We Know It?*, CSHE Research & Occasional Paper Series (University of California, Berkley: 2005), http://www.cshe.berkeley.edu/sites/default/files/shared/publications/docs/ROP.Cross.7.05.pdf

Diamond, J. B. "Where the Rubber Meets the Road: Rethinking the Connection Between High-Stakes Testing Policy and Classroom Instruction." *Sociology of Education* 80 (4) (2007): 285-313

Speak Up 2014 National Research Project Findings: Flipped Learning Continues to Trend for Third Year (Project Tomorrow and Flipped Learning Network, 2016), http://flippedlearning.org/wp-content/uploads/2016/07/Speak-Up-FLN-2014-Survey-Results-FINAL.pdf

Talbert, Robert, How Much Research Has Been Done on Flipped Learning? (2016), http://rtalbert.org/blog/2016/how-much-research

---

JON BERGMANN *is a chemistry teacher and one of the developers of the "flipped classroom" model of teaching along with fellow chemistry teacher Aaron Sams. Although already noted for his teaching, Bergmann decided to "flip" what students did in his classes, watching video lectures at home and doing exercises (homework) in class under supervision. He and Sams not only found that grades went up, they also realized time for other types of activities, which Bergmann states is more important than the videos. Bergmann has since became the lead technology facilitator for a school in Illinois and has worked to promote the models speaking at schools, universities, and more both in the United States and abroad.*

Bergmann worked in education for over twenty-six years, spending twenty-four years as a middle and high school science teacher. He first taught for three years at Baker Middle School, than a year at Englewood High School before moving on to Eaglecrest High School, south of Denver, Colorado, where he taught for fifteen years. This was then followed by a position at Woodland Park High School teaching with traditional methods for four years. Later, along with fellow chemistry teacher Aaron Sams, he experimented with putting lectures on video for students to view outside of class. He then became the lead technology facilitator for the Joseph Sears School in Kenilworth, Illinois. Today, Bergmann is dedicated to writing, speaking, and otherwise promoting the flipped classroom concept.

15

Digital Equity is the Civil Rights Issue of Our Time

Keith Krueger and Jayne James

There's a Problem

The growing ubiquity of Internet access and pervasive use of online information has changed the learning landscape forever. Students continue to benefit from enhanced connectivity throughout the formal school day thanks to a $1,500,000,000 increase in E-Rate funding in late 2014. However, demand and expectations for learning *outside* of the school day are on the rise, and there are still many students struggling to complete homework online.

Successfully completed homework and Flipped Classroom learning are directly dependent upon access within the home at best, or throughout the community if a home connection isn't currently available. Broadband access and adoption in cities, regional communities, and small towns continue to lag for certain population segments, including low-income, and rural communities. This is referred to as the digital divide—i.e., *the gap between people who have access to broadband services, and know how to use the internet, and those who do not have such access or knowledge.*[1]

In a 2013 American Consumer Survey, ten cities with a population of over 100,000 denoted that approximately a third of their population had no broadband access in the home. Detroit topped the list with 39.9 percent of its residents not connected, followed with incrementally better connection rates by Miami, Cleveland, New Orleans, Buffalo, Memphis, St. Louis, Milwaukee, Baltimore, and Cincinnati, which faired a bit better than the other nine, with a 30.3 percent non-connection rate.[2]

The Pew Research Center conducted an analysis of the 2013 American Community Survey by the U.S. Census Bureau revealed that an estimated 5,000,000,000 households with school-age children do not have high-speed Internet service at home. Low-income households, especially Black and Hispanic households, make up a disproportionate share of that 5,000,000,000.[3] The under-connection of low-income families is a real issue. Clearly, there is a great deal of work that needs to be done to narrow this inequitable gap. This issue constitutes a new civil right; the right to connect to needed resources—anywhere, anytime; the right to digital equity. This is a civil right that cannot be achieved by school leaders alone. A holistic approach will ensure that school-aged children aren't reduced to little or no access. It calls for community leadership; connected and collaborative leadership.

Federal Communications Commissioner Jessica Rosenworcel defines the gap this way: "Data suggests seven in ten teachers now assign homework that requires internet access. But, the Federal Communications Commission's (FCC) data about broadband says that one in three households doesn't have access to the Internet. So, think about where those numbers overlap because that's the homework gap."[4] A 2014 report by the Alliance for Excellent Education and the Stanford Center for Opportunity Policy in Education found that teachers in high-poverty schools were more than twice as likely to say that their students' lack of access to technology outside of school posed a challenge in their classrooms. Only 3 percent of teachers in high-poverty schools said that their students had the digital tools necessary to complete homework assignments while at home, compared to 52 percent of teachers in more affluent schools.[5]

When President Obama announced the ConnectED initiative in 2013, only thirty percent of school districts had access to high-speed broadband. Today, 20,000,000 more students have access to high-speed broadband in their classrooms, and according to the Future Ready initiative blog, the United States is on track to have ninety-nine percent of students with access by 2018.[6] School leaders have been very focused on providing robust access on school campuses, and buildings, yet providing solutions for out of school connections are still an enormous challenge. In a 2014 Consortium for School Networking (CoSN) survey, nearly 75 percent of school systems surveyed did not have any off campus strategies for providing connectivity to students at home and after school.[7]

If you were to simply ask lower-income families if they had Wi-Fi and a device, the majority would say yes. However, the Joan Ganz Cooney Center, a team of researchers funded by the Bill and Melinda Gates Foundation, who undertook just such a mission, reported that "access to the Internet and digital devices is no longer a simple yes/no question. Whether families have consistent quality connections and the capabilities to make the most of being connected is becoming just as important." Further, according to their first-of-its-kind nationally representative survey of 1,191 low- and moderate- income parents with school-aged children (ages six to thirteen), among families who have home Internet access, half (52 percent) say their access is too slow, one quarter (26 percent) say too many people share the same computer, and one fifth (20 percent) say their Internet has been cut off in the last year due to lack of payment.[8]

Despite these inequities, there is also good news. This chapter states the case for why this issue is so pressing, and shines a light on pioneering educators working in this space with others to lessen the gap. They are collaborating to provide three key components for digital equity within the community:

1. **Computing devices**—Many students and parents have smart phones, yet it is tedious and for some, impossible to read, write, and interact with several digital learning resources, and limits on family data plans can be an issue as well.

2. **Broadband access at school, home and within the community**—It's imperative to have access to connect with learning resources provided on the Internet.

3. **Services to ensure community members have digital literacy skills**—Students and parents need basic skills on how to connect with pertinent content, interact with others, and how to search for and find needed resources.

Why It Matters

"Google it!" That's the action most millennials take when they have a question. Whether they need to know pertinent information for formal learning, how to fix a leaky faucet, or seek advice on where to eat dinner, the ever-present access to the Internet and digital literacy skills give them a distinct learning advantage. And millennials are not alone. Google now processes over 40,000 search queries every second on average, which translates to over 3,500,000,000 searches per day, and 1,200,000,000,000 searches per year worldwide.[9] That's a lot; and that number is infinitely on the grow! With that growth, come the threat and reality of the widening gap for those who currently do not have access nor have the ability to connect.

Connectivity matters. From a career and economic development standpoint, businesses are in search of digitally literate employees. In fact, almost every job application now requires an application to be completed online, so a person needs this skillset to even be considered for an entry level position. Basic government services have shifted online, as well as utilities and housing applications. There is a strong need for all citizens to be digitally literate, and having a smart phone to check sports scores on ESPN, or checking a Weather App, doesn't necessarily prepare someone for digital literacy.

Retrofitting adults into a digital economy is of great importance, yet it is imperative for adults to understand how critical digital access is for their children. Technology has transformed how parents spend leisure time at home if they have access to social media, and entertainment on demand through cable or another home entertainment service. Today's parents of infants, preschoolers and students in the PK-12 system were more than likely born after 1980, and are considered to be the world's earliest "digital natives." They value being connected, yet it may be hard for them to consider how vital it is to provide Internet access in the home for their children to use separately from their phone service. Developmentally, it's not uncommon for a two-year-old to now attempt to "click, drag or pinch" electronic screens, as they intuitively navigate entertainment and learning devices, yet it's quite another task to ask a school-aged child to complete a homework assignment using mom's, dad's, or a grandparent's phone. Providing tablets, laptops and desktops to families in need is a priority of many schools and community partners.

The rapid acceleration and adoption of digital content for learning is a pressing catalyst for digital equity. A CoSN 2016 IT Leadership Survey reports that at least 50 percent of learning resources and content are expected to be digital within the next three years.[10] A 2015 Survey of by ASCD and One Drive cite that 80 percent of administrators surveyed are using some type of digital content within their schools with another 9 percent planning to implement digital content in the next year or so. Administrators responded that the top three benefits from using digital content were: the ability to deliver individualized instruction; allowing students to practice independently; and capturing greater student attention/engagement, empowering students to take charge of their own learning.[11]

Demand matters. Online courses have become a standard offering at district, state, national, and international levels. In 2000, it is estimated that 45,000 K-12 students participated in online courses. It is estimated that 3,000,000 students took an online course in 2009, and it is predicted that by 2019, 50 percent of high school classes will be delivered online.[12] When YouTube hit the online airwaves in 2005, no one had any idea how viral the idea of posting and sharing videos would become. Today, YouTube users view over 40,000,000,000 videos per day, and it reaches more 18-49 year olds than any cable network in the United States.[13] Easy access to free content and the ability to easy-post has allowed this platform to grow from simply hosting cat videos and other home-grown entertainment to becoming a legitimate resource for learning, regardless of viewers' ages.

Kids matter. The quality of families' Internet connections and the kinds and capabilities of devices they can access have considerable consequences for parents and children alike.[14] As more and more schools embrace a personalized or blended approach to learning, connectivity is essential. Digital equity is essential. The right to connect to needed resources—anywhere, anytime is a civil right they richly deserve. It empowers students to drive relevance, build confidence, take pride in their achievements, and quite often, exceed teacher and parent expectations!

Although school leadership is challenged in providing comprehensive Internet at home and throughout the community, 42 percent of administrators surveyed by CoSN in the fall of 2016 addressed Digital equity and lack of broadband access outside of school as a very high priority focus area.[15] They want to ensure that students can bridge the homework gap wherever and whenever they choose to learn. Leaders realize this issue is big. It's an issue that cannot be solved in isolation. They are turning to the power of collaboration and key partnerships to get kids and their families the connectivity they need and deserve.

Digital Equity Leadership in Action

Today, we see innovative leaders and students from schools working in collaboration with community leaders and organizations to narrow the access gap and bring digital equity to their communities. Collectively, they have a greater capacity to gather and leverage resources to provide creative and effective solutions to the gap. Every community differs in size, yet it needs to be inclusive and expansive when considering potential partners when goal setting for digital equity. The simple definition of community is a group of people who live in the same area such as a city, town, or neighborhood.[16] They assemble loosely or through established structure. They have similar interests, religion, race, or perhaps… goals for digital equity. And who might community leaders be? Certainly local or state government officials, yet the list can be extensive. Schools can tap into public-private partnerships that are already established: the local chamber of commerce, corporations and individual businesses, community-based organizations, community and religious leaders, parents and certainly, don't rule out students! There are also a number of Federal programs happening in agencies separately from the U.S. Department of Education which are also tackling the issue of connectivity.

Let's take a look at some brief snapshots of community leadership in action on behalf of Digital Equity. To learn more, follow the links provided at the end of this chapter.

District and Mayoral Partnership—MA

Paul Dakin, Superintendent of Revere Public Schools teamed up with Mayor Daniel Rizzo to accomplish together what individual agencies might not have been able to achieve alone. Strategies identified to address digital equity include: allowing computer labs access before and after school, working with the public library to provide community access and literacy programs, and working with community businesses to get their businesses online. Revere was recognized as one of three winning cities for their student-led effort in the Getting Your Business Online Competition.

Students, Parents, District, University and Community Effort—NC

In Charlotte-Mecklenburg School District in North Carolina, students are playing a major role in igniting a community-wide effort to provide student access to both computers and broadband outside of the school day. Franny Millen is only 13, but she's already created her own nonprofit that is closing the digital divide in Davidson and Cornelius, NC. She quickly and convincingly partnered with parents, her school district, the mayor, and corporations in addition to school leaders, and a lot of it began with sales from student-led lemonade stands! E2D, Eliminate the Digital Divide, a non-profit organization has been formed, and together, their collective impact is making strong headway.

Community-Based Organization—MO and KS

Connecting for Good has been bridging the digital divide since 2011, and is the only Kansas City area nonprofit that has digital inclusion as its core mission. Local school districts can benefit from partnering with a local organization such as this. It provides wireless mesh networks (an ad hoc network that can be created by connecting other existing networks), community technology centers, low cost refurbished personal computers, and free digital life skills classes. They believe that connectivity equals opportunity. Their website states that "Access to the Internet brings with it a chance to apply for jobs online, connections with family and friends, access to virtual library shelves, information about medical and health issues, online education—GED completion and college courses—and a whole lot more."[17]

National Corporate Partners

There are many examples of how national and international corporations are stepping up in partnership with community leaders to provide services, yet Google Fiber perhaps has taken the boldest of steps in providing inclusive and super-fast Internet to a select number of cities throughout the country. Google offers a connection speed of up to one gigabit per second (1,000 Mbit/s) for both download and upload which is roughly 100 times faster access than what most Americans have within their homes. Kansas City was first—then Google Fiber announced expansion to Austin, Texas, and Provo, Utah, in April 2013, and subsequent expansions in 2014 and 2015 to Atlanta, Charlotte, Raleigh–Durham, Nashville, Salt Lake City, and San Antonio.[18] Services have even included the wiring, and training for families living within public housing units within select Google Fiber cities.

Federal Government Initiatives

The E-Rate program provided by the Federal Communications Commission has been assisting schools and libraries with infrastructure and Internet costs for almost 20 years. In June 2013, President Obama announced the ConnectED initiative, designed to enrich K-12 education for every student in America. ConnectED empowers teachers with the best technology and the training to make the most of it, and empowers students through individualized learning and rich, digital content. The Future Ready Movement within the Office of Educational Technology at the U.S. Department of Education is focusing on helping K-12 public, private and charter school leaders plan and implement personalized, research-based digital learning strategies so all student can achieve their full potential. Although these programs primarily affect learning within the classroom day, with digital learning and a personalized approach students need access before and after school as well. There are other federal agencies tackling the issue of connectivity outside of the classroom. For example:

- ■ **Connect Home—Designed to build regional partnerships**
  The Department of Housing and Urban Development (HUD) is collaborating with EveryoneOn and US Ignite who worked with private- and public-sector leaders to build local partnerships, and gather commitments that will increase access to the Internet for low-income Americans. These partnerships will bring broadband, technical assistance and digital literacy training to students living in public and assisted housing across America.
- ■ **Lifeline—Modernizing for the Digital Age**
  Since 1985, the Lifeline program has provided a discount on phone service for qualifying low-income consumers to ensure that all Americans have the opportunities and security that phone service brings, including being able to connect to jobs, family and emergency services. Lifeline is part of the Universal Service Fund. The Lifeline program is available to eligible low-income consumers in every state, territory, commonwealth, and on Tribal lands. In the 2016 Lifeline

Modernization Order, the Commission included broadband as a support service in the Lifeline program.

What You Can Do

Wanting to get started on digital equity today? Here are four, concrete actions-steps you can take immediately to get underway:

1. **Survey, survey, survey!** Assess what's available within the community and take stock: school by school, local libraries, family by family, to find out what kinds of devices, if any, people have at home and what kind of connectivity they have;

2. **Engage your community.** Get together with other educators, as well as community and business leaders and philanthropists to brainstorm and develop community solutions for closing the homework gap;

3. **Ensure sustainability through community assets.** Partners must work together to ensure that the energy to address digital equity now has long-term staying power, and see to it they leverage every opportunity available throughout the community;

4. **Consider out of the box solutions, and rethink how connectivity could be accessed.** For example, the Coachella Valley Unified School District in California, one of the poorest districts in the nation, provides Wi-Fi on its school busses. The busses, equipped with solar panels, are parked overnight in the most underserved communities so that students can have internet access 24/7.[19]

Further detail with these action steps are offered in the CoSN Digital Equity Toolkit, yet summarizing tips are resources are offered.[20]

Surveys

Surveys can help you identify the scope of the problem in providing digital equity outside of the school day. In other words, it is important for district and school leadership to be able to fully articulate the context for digital learning that their students engage in outside of school. Teachers and school administrators may be generally aware of digital equity challenges within the district and may even know specific students who have limited access to the Internet outside of the classroom. It is crucial, however, for districts to broaden this awareness with survey data. No need to reinvent the wheel. Here are three surveys that you can connect with to either implement as is, or to gain insight from if your team insists on creating a survey unique to your community:

- American Community Survey[21]—The American Community Survey is conducted by the U.S. Census bureau and helps local officials, community leaders, and businesses understand the changes taking place in their communities. It is the premier source for detailed information about the American people and workforce.

- CoSN and The Friday Institute for Educational Innovation at North Carolina State University have created a set of recommended student and parent survey questions available free to districts in the appendix of the Digital Equity Toolkit[22]. These surveys are valuable tools for districts to understand and track progress in addressing digital equity challenges and identify emerging issues. Suggested categories for questions to include in a survey? Ask about devices, places, and speed of connectivity.

- The Grundy School District in Iowa[23] neatly incorporates out-of-school connectivity into their technology planning effort. Collecting this data allowed the district to understand the nature of out-of-school connectivity experienced by students within the district's elementary school, middle school, and high school.

Engage Your Community

Your government, community, and civic leaders are most certainly a must-connect as you work for digital equity outside of the school day, yet do your homework before reaching out. Perhaps the community is already meeting in a formalized way. Have they already made a commitment to advancing digital equity? As you begin planning your own digital equity strategies, take stock of efforts that are already underway, and identify areas where coordination makes sense. This will enable the entire community to make the best use of local resources, and to better serve its members. Earlier, we mentioned a list of community members you could potentially partner with, yet the Open Technology Institute (OTI) provides excellent guidance on the process of engaging partners across the community in digital equity initiatives. OTI has identified a list of partners who can play a critical role in the long-term sustainability of neighborhood technology investments.[24]

There are also several national organizations and associations actively working with communities in providing digital equity:

- EveryoneOn—EveryoneOn is a national nonprofit working to eliminate the digital divide by making high-speed, low-cost Internet service and computers, and free digital literacy courses accessible to all unconnected Americans.[25]

- National Digital Inclusion Alliance (NDIA) is a unified voice for local technology training, home broadband access, and public broadband access programs. The alliance works collaboratively to craft, identify, and disseminate financial and operational resources for digital inclusion programs while serving as a bride to policy makers and the public.[26]

- Next Century Cities—supports community leaders across the country as they seek to ensure that all have access to fast, affordable, and reliable Internet. They work with mayors, local government officials, as well as state and national digital equity initiatives.[27]

- PCs for People—a nonprofit organization that is an electronics recycler striving to bridge the digital divide by providing the necessary tools to put a functional computer into the hands of low-income individuals and get them online. They fulfill their mission through partnerships and have over 250 business and government agencies to recycle and refurbish their retired electronics.[28]

Ensure Sustainability of Community Assets

It's never too early to identify and begin enacting strategies to ensure that your work is sustained across leadership organization. Here are two examples of how you might leverage community assets on a regional level to build sustainable digital equity solutions.

- Chippewa Valley Internetworking Consortium (CINC)— Formed in 1999, CINC is a regional Community Area Network (CAN) committed to "broadband serving the public interest." It became an Unincorporated Association in 2011 and coordinates regional communication infrastructure projects with city, county, and state government, educational institutions, libraries, hospitals, health care, nonprofits, and technology providers to facilitate and create innovative, competitive, and sustainable networks.[29]

- Public broadcasting stations are leveraging their educational broadcasting spectrums to partner with Sprint to bring broadband to low income families for educational purposes. South Carolina, Missouri, and California have interesting and helpful examples to offer.

Consider Out-Of-The-Box Solutions and Rethink How Connectivity Could be Accessed

As we connect all households—especially the poorest ones—to broadband, there are tremendous opportunities to bring in other community partners. We need to think creatively. On a CoSN delegation to Uruguay, we saw how their one-to-one program, Plan Ceibal, which sends a school device home, also delivers nutrition programs for mothers after the children go to bed.[30] Are you reaching out to other agencies and nonprofits with missions to advance the health and employment of low-income families?

There are several examples of how creative connectivity is enhancing the lives of students outside of their school day, and Internet WI-FI and hotspots are becoming a key part of the equation, and although some may view this as more novel than impactful, Huntsville, Alabama is seeing results. Connectivity on buses appears to reduce behavioral problems, as students focus more on their screens, and less on creating disturbances. Huntsville City Schools reported a 70 percent drop in discipline problems after installing hotspots on their buses.[31] This can increase district costs, but gives students more learning and homework time, and it adds up fast: based on a 30-minute bus ride, this represents 30 more school days per year of potential time-on-task. Consider these approaches as you lay the collaborative groundwork with your community collaboration:

- Wi-Fi zones offered within the community provided by community businesses or corporate partners focused where students and families spend time: laundry mats, the public library, fast food restaurants, and shopping districts;

- Mobile hotspots offered to students who may be unable to attend school for long periods of time. Kajeet has been a valued partner to schools in this area, along with mobile service providers; and
- Take advantage of special broadband offerings. Most broadband carriers have discounted rates for low income families within their service areas.

Together We're Better

You realize providing access to key digital resources outside of the school day is quickly becoming a necessity. This is a tall order. Don't tackle this task in isolation. Most of the examples offered within this chapter started as bubble-up efforts by collaborative groups—many of them students—cobbling together whatever they could to provide connectivity outside the school day. Tap into existing efforts that are happening within your local communities or use the CoSN toolkit to get community conversations underway. The power of collaboration and the leveraging of existing assets will take you further, faster! However the tasks unfold, the digital equity journey you embark upon will be of value for students and the community!

Link to School Leadership in Action

1. MA: Paul Dakin, Superintendent of Revere Public Schools teamed up with Mayor Daniel Rizzo http://www.cosn.org/blogwhy-working-class-revere-massachusetts-cares-about-digital-equity
2. MA: Getting Your Business Online Competition Winning You Tube Video (Revere Public Schools) https://www.youtube.com/watch?v=yGZWxdFff4Y
3. NC: Students, Parents, District, University and Community Effort, Charlotte Mecklenburg School District http://www.cms.k12.nc.us/News/Pages/Student%E2%80%99snonprofitaimstobridgedigitaldivide.aspx
4. NC: E2D, Eliminate the Digital Divide Non-Profit Organization (Student Founded in Charlotte Mecklenburg Community) http://www.e-2-d.org/

Learn more about federal programs working to provide digital equity

1. E-Rate Universal Service Fund https://www.fcc.gov/general/e-rate-schools-libraries-usf-program
2. ConnectED Initiative—The White House https://www.whitehouse.gov/issues/education/k-12/connected
3. Future Ready Schools http://tech.ed.gov/futureready/ and http://futureready.org/
4. Connect Home; A Public Private Partnership to Narrow the Digital Divide http://connecthome.hud.gov
5. Lifeline https://www.fcc.gov/general/lifeline-program-low-income-consumers

References

1. Levin, Blair, Denise Linn, *The Next Generation Network Connectivity Handbook: A Guide for Community Leaders Seeking Affordable, Abundant Bandwidth* (Benton Foundation, 2015) www.gig-u.org/cms/assets/uploads/2015/07/Val-NexGen_design_7.9_ v2.pdf.

2. Barton, Jordana, *Closing the Digital Divide: A Framework for Meeting CRA Obligations* (Federal Reserve Bank of Dallas, San Antonio Branch, 2016) https://dallasfed.org/assets/documents/cd/pubs/digitaldivide.pdf.

3. *Pew Research Center analysis of the U.S. Census Bureau, 2013 American Community Survey.* http://www.pewresearch.org/fact-tank/2015/04/20/the-numbers-behind-the-broadband-homework-gap/

4. Cruz, Mimi Ko, Watchworthy Wednesday (DML, 2016) http://dmlcentral.net/watchworthy-wednesday-closing-homework-gap/?utm_source=maillist.uci. edu&utm_medium=email&utmcampaign=Watchworthy%2BOctober

5. Darling-Hammond, Linda, Molly B. Zielezinski, Shelley Goldman, *Using Technology to Support at Risk Students' Learning* (Alliance for Excellent Education and the Stanford Center for Opportunity Policy in Education, 2014) https://edpolicy.stanford.edu/sites/default/files/scope-pub-using-technology-report.pdf

6. Future Ready—ConnectED Day, September, 2016, http://futureready.org/connected/
7. CoSN, CoSN's 2015 *Annual E-Rate and Infrastructure Survey* (CoSN, 2015) http://cosn.org/sites/default/files/pdf/CoSN_3rd_Annual_Survey_Oct15_FINALV2.pdf
8. Joan Ganz Cooney Center, *Digital Equity* http://digitalequityforlearning.org
9. Google Statistics http://www.internetlivestats.com/google-search-statistics/
10. *CoSN 2016 IT Leadership Survey Report* http://www.cosn.org/itsurvey
11. ASCD and OverDrive Inc., *Digital Content Goes to School: Trends in K-12 Classroom e-Learning* (ASCD and OverDrive, 2014) http://www.ascd.org/ASCD/pdf/siteASCD/misc/DigitalContentTrendsReport.pdf
12. Horn, Michael B., Heather Staker, The Rise of Blended Learning (Innosight Institute, 2011) http://www.christensen-institute.org/wp-content/uploads/2013/04/The-rise-of-K-12-blended-learning.pdf
13. DMR, http://expandedramblings.com/index.php/youtube-statistics/
14. Rideout, Victoria, Vikki S. Katz, *Opportunity for All? Technology and Learning in Lower-Income Families* (Joan Ganz Cooney Foundation, 2016) http://www.joanganzcooneycenter.org/wp-content/uploads/2016/01/jgcc_opportunityforall.pdf
15. *CoSN 2016 IT Leadership Survey Report* http://www.cosn.org/itsurvey
16. "Community" in Merriam-Webster Dictionary http://merriam-webster.com/dictionary/community
17. *Connecting for Good* http://www.connectingforgood.org/about/
18. Google Fiber https://en.wikipedia.org/wiki/Google_Fiber
19. *WI-FI Powered Buses* 24/7 http://tech.ed.gov/assessment/leaders/?action=full-video-library&videoId=YZNGz-qiVHE
20. *CoSN Digital Equity Toolkit: Supporting Students and Families in Out of School Learning* http://cosn.org/focus-areas/leadership-vision/digital-equity-action-agenda

21. *American Community Survey* https://www.census.gov/programs-surveys/acs/

22. *CoSN Digital Equity Toolkit: Supporting Students and Families in Out of School Learning* http://cosn.org/focus-areas/leadership-vision/digital-equity-action-agenda

23. *Grundy School District Technology Plan* https://sites.google.com/a/spartanpride.net/grundy-center-technology-plan/home

24. Open Technology Institute—list can be found within the CoSN Digital Equity Toolkit http://cosn.org/focus-areas/leadership-vision/digital-equity-action-agenda

25. *EveryoneOn* http://everyoneon.org/

26. National Digital Inclusion Alliance http://www.digitalinclusionalliance.org/

27. Next Century Cities http://nextcenturycities.org/

28. PCs for People http://pcsforpeople.com/

29. Chippewa Internetworking Consortium https://cincua.org

30. Plan Ceibal https://cosnintltrips.wordpress.com/2011/11/11/visiting-plan-ceibal/

31. *AL.com Wi-Fi on Buses helps bus discipline reports drop 70% for Huntsville City School; more Wi-Fi planned for 2015-16* http://www.al.com/news/huntsville/index.ssf/2015/04/wi-fi_leads_to_70_drop_in_bus.html

KEITH KRUEGER *is the Chief Executive Officer of CoSN, the Consortium for School Networking in Washington, D.C., and* **JAYNE JAMES** *Directs the CoSN Digital Equity Action Agenda.*